The Complete

Dried Fruit Cookbook

To Cheryl & family wishing you all good health always & a fun time with the recipes

Boon.
S'pore 27/1/05

R&R PUBLICATIONS

ANGAS PARK

The possibilities are endless...

Major Credits

Published by:
R&R Publications Marketing Pty Ltd
ACN 083 612 579
PO Box 254, Carlton North, Victoria 3054 Australia
Australia-wide toll free 1800 063 296

©Richard Carroll
Publisher: Richard Carroll
Project Manager: David Keats (Angas Park)
Promotions Manager: Joanne Van Eunen (Angas Park)
Food Photography: Garry Smith
Food Stylist: Janet Lodge
Assistants: Christina Panteli and Caroline Jones
Recipe Development: Ellen Argyriou
Creative Director: Jon Terpstra
Layout: Jenny Ring
Editor/Proofreader: Jenny Ring

The National Library of Australia
Cataloguing-in-Publication Data.
Argyriou, Ellen
    Cooking with Dried Fruits
    Includes index.
    ISBN 1 875655 87 5
    1. Cookery (Dried Fruit). 1. Title
641.614

First edition printed February 1999
Computer typeset in Esprit, Baskerville and Veljovic by:
R&R Publications Marketing, Brunswick, Victoria,
    Australia
Printed by APP Printing, Singapore
Film Scanning by PICA Overseas, Singapore

The Publishers would like to acknowledge and thank the
Angas Park Fruit Company Pty Ltd for their support and
assistance with the provision of materials for photography
and the produce for photography and recipe development.

Contents

Angas Park

COMPANY PROFILE

Angas Park Fruit Company Pty Ltd is a privately-owned family company, situated in the heritage-rich Barossa Valley of South Australia.

The Company was established in 1911 by Julius Wilhelm Mattiske. Over the years, because of an uncompromising commitment to quality, variety and presentation, Angas Park has grown into the most successful dried fruit company in Australia.

Angas Park is the focal point for the country's finest produce, from over 1,500 growers in South Australia's Barossa Valley and Riverland, Victoria's Sunraysia and New South Wales' Riverina, with a total marketing programme of over 15,000 tonnes of dried fruit each year.

The dedicated workforce of over 300 full time and 700 seasonal employees inspires an aggressive marketing philosophy, which has continued the growth of the company's customer loyalty base, resulting in over a 100-fold increase in turnover in the past 20 years.

The distinctive retail packs are available in all of Australia's retail chains and health food outlets, where they have a market share of over 40% of Australian dried fruit sales. In addition to retail sales Angas Park is a major supplier to the baking, confectionery and breakfast cereal industry and continues to develop their export marketing which currently supplies twenty overseas countries.

Angas Park fruit is particularly appealing as it is grown and processed in a pollution-free environment. The natural and traditional art of drying fruit is one of the few preserving processes in which the natural flavour and nutritional value of the fruit is not destroyed by modern processing and refining methods. The drying process concentrates the nutrients of fresh fruit, and allows us to enjoy the benefit of fruit all year round.

Gawler Park Fruits, a glacé fruit manufacturer and marketer, was purchased by Angas Park in 1991. The philosophies and directions that have fuelled Angas Park's success are now being applied to Gawler Park, as we introduce the world market to the finest quality Australian glacé apricots, peaches, pears, figs, apples, quince, pineapple and orange.

For further information contact the Angas Park Fruit Company Pty Ltd, 3 Murray Street, Angaston, South Australia 5353, or visit our web site at **www.angaspark.com.au**.

NUTRITIONAL INFORMATION PER 100g OF PRODUCT

Product	Energy (kj)	Protein (g)	Fat (g)	Total Carbo-hydrate (g)	Total Sugars (g)	Sodium (mg)	Potassium (mg)
Sultanas	1276	2.8	0.4	75.0	73.2	36	910
Currants	1143	1.9	0.5	72.8	58.2	21	719
Raisins	1168	1.5	0.5	74.9	59.7	49	840
Dried Apricots	1110	4.5	0.4	68.3	49.8	23	1561
Dried Peaches	1101	3.2	0.7	68.5	52.1	11.0	1191
Dried Pears	1130	1.2	1.8	70	56.7	7.0	573
Prunes	1057	2.8	0.3	59.9	43.8	11.6	673
Dried Fruit Salad	1070	2.4	1.0	67	53.6	10.0	890
Dried Fruit Medley	1136	2.6	0.8	71.2	57.0	22	1009

Introduction

Australians usually associate dried fruits with glorious winter puddings, rich moist fruit cakes, fruit loaves and buns, and festive occasions such as Christmas and weddings. In writing this book, I wanted to explore the wider use of dried fruits in cooking. To do this, my research took me a long way back in time.

Early in our civilisation, the people of Mesopotamia discovered that the forgotten grapes left on the vines, which had shrivelled and dried, had a concentrated and appealing flavour. They realised that the dried grapes were easily portable, and they took them for sustenance when travelling across the vast land. Man's first convenient food had arrived.

The Ancient Egyptians dried their grapes by burying them in the hot sand, the Ancient Greeks spread their grapes and figs on trestles in the hot sun. We also know that they used dried raisins to make the thick, sweet wine "gordo". As time passed the Greeks began to kneed sultanas into their yeast breads.

In my research, I found inspiration from the foods enjoyed by the Ancient Kings of Persia and the Caliphs of Baghdad who, centuries later, had expanded the cuisine inherited from earlier times. They enjoyed the taste of the "exotic" in their food, and their cooks did not hesitate in combining dried peaches, pears, apricots and prunes with meat, chicken and rice in their recipes.

This exotic cuisine travelled with merchants through the Middle East and North Africa. The Crusaders were thought to be the bridge which took this culinary concept to Europe. Dried prunes, apples and apricots began to appear in meat and poultry dishes throughout Europe and into the New World.

My task of developing the recipes in this book was assisted greatly by the exceptional quality of the Angas Park dried fruits. The fruits are dried to the required degree for preservation, yet still have a tender, moist texture and full flavour. A simple sautéed steak with a few Angas Park peaches or pears, quickly sautéed in the pan juices, will make a meal fit for a Persian King.

Throughout the pages of this book you will be able to find "Something" for everyone and "Something" for all occasions.

Ellen Argyriou

Dried Fruits

APRICOTS

Trevatt, Moorpark, Hunter, Watkins and Story apricots are just some of the varieties of apricots used for drying. The fruit is picked "eating ripe" and graded into sizes.

The fruit is cut and stone removed, then placed onto trays for drying. The trays with apricots are then placed in the sun until the correct dehydration is reached.

Dried apricot consumption is second after sultanas and is a popular snacking food. Apricots have a very extensive culinary use, being used in stuffing for turkey and chicken, mixed with nuts into rice dishes, popped into casseroles and stews, as well as desserts and baked products.

CURRANTS

The Zanta Currant and Carina grapes are used for making currants. They are placed onto drying racks and are shaded from direct sunlight, as with sultanas.

Currants are not as common as the other vine fruits. Their main use is in fruit puddings and fruit cakes. Several delightful recipes for savoury dishes using currants are included in this book.

PEACHES

Freestone peaches are only used for drying. Varieties used are Elberta, Blackburn, Hale and Halehaven. They are picked when well coloured but still firm. Peaches are cut and placed on trays like apricots, before being placed in direct sunlight for two to three days. The trays are then stacked and placed in a shaded area until the fruit is dried.

Dried peaches have an intense and appealing flavour and can be enjoyed as is. They are included in puddings, desserts and cakes and are delicious when sautéed and served with grilled chicken and meats.

PEARS

The William Bon Chretion variety of pears is the only one used for drying, because it is the only variety of pear which is ready for picking in the summer months. The pears are picked while still firm and are fully ripened in boxes, covered to exclude light. They are halved and the calyx is removed, before being exposed to the sun for one to three days. Drying is finished in the shade.

Sun dried pears are an appealing snack food, and are used in simple puddings. Their mild, sweet flavour and chewy texture complement vegetable dishes, salads and chicken dishes.

PRUNES

The d'Agen and Robe de Sargaent plums are the varieties mostly used for making into prunes. The plums are picked ripe and are placed onto trays, and dried in dehydration tunnels. The prunes are then exposed to direct sunlight.

A popular use of prunes is with cereals for breakfast. They are included in puddings, pies and cakes and are very complementary to pork, both fresh and cured. Prunes are the "plums" in old-fashioned plum pudding.

RAISINS

The Muscat Gordo Blanco and the Walthan Cross grapes are the varieties used in producing raisins. They are large grapes with a rich, full flavour. The grapes are dehydrated in a special "racks dehydrator" where hot air of 60°C is forced over the fruit.

The rich flavour of raisins favours their inclusion in baked products as well as meat dishes, curries, chutney and salads.

SULTANAS

Sultanas are made from the Sultana and Thompson Seedless grapes. The grapes are placed on drying racks shaded from direct sunlight, where the warm air can flow through the racks, ensuring slow, even drying.

Sultana consumption is the highest of all the dried fruits. They are used in cakes, puddings, breads and buns, as well as being included in many savoury dishes. Sultanas are a popular snack food for people of all ages.

Something Simple

The versatility of dried fruits is demonstrated by how simple they are to use—their addition not only complements many foods, but also adds nutritional balance. Simple snacks, salads and sandwich fillings, as well as accompaniments to cold meats, are featured in this chapter.

Photographed from bottom left, clockwise: Quick Fruit Chutney, recipe page 10; Raisin and Carrot Salad, recipe page 10; Spiced Peaches, recipe page 10; Lemon Ginger Pears in Green Salad, recipe page 11; Fruit Cheese with Brandy, recipe page 11.

Raisin and Carrot Salad

INGREDIENTS

3 medium-sized carrots

2 tbsp *Angas Park Seeded Raisins*

2 tbsp orange juice

½ tbsp butter

Wash, peel and coarsely grate the carrots. Place in a shallow pie plate, stir in the raisins, sprinkle with orange juice and dot with butter.

Cover with a plate or plastic wrap, pierce wrap once. Cook in a microwave on high for 3 minutes. Serve hot as an accompaniment to a main course.

TIP

This dish may be served cold—microwave for only 2 minutes, allow to cool and then chill in the refrigerator.

Spiced Peaches

INGREDIENTS

1 cup water

¼ cup vinegar

½ cup brown sugar

4cm piece cinnamon stick

2cm piece fresh ginger or 1 tsp ground ginger

Place water, vinegar, sugar and all the spices in a saucepan, bring to the boil then simmer, uncovered, for 10 minutes, until a thickish syrup.

Place peaches in a bowl, pour over the hot syrup. Cover and chill several hours or overnight (they can be stored in the refrigerator for up to 4 days). Serve with cold ham, pork, turkey or other deli meats.

INGREDIENTS CONT.

1 tsp allspice

3 black peppercorns

2 cloves

1 x 200g packet *Angas Park Peaches*

Quick Fruit Chutney

INGREDIENTS

150g (1 cup) *Angas Park Fruit Medley*

1 cup boiling water

¼ cup brown sugar

Place the fruit medley in a straight-sided microwave-safe bowl or jug. Add boiling water and stand for 5 minutes. Microwave on high 2 minutes. Stir in sugar, make sure it has dissolved, then add all remaining ingredients. Microwave on high 8 minutes, stirring twice during cooking. Cool and serve with cold meats.

INGREDIENTS CONT.

¼ cup vinegar

½ cinnamon stick

⅛ tsp mixed spice

¼ tsp ground ginger

Fruit Cheese with Brandy

INGREDIENTS

2 *Angas Park Pears*

3 *Angas Park Peaches*

10 *Angas Park Fancy Large Apricots*

30g (¼ cup) *Angas Park Seeded Raisins*

30g (¼ cup) *Angas Park Sultanas*

¼ cup sugar

¼ cup brandy

500g cream cheese

Snip the pears, peaches, apricots and raisins into small pieces with a pair of kitchen scissors. Place in a screw-top jar with the sultanas, sprinkle with sugar and add the brandy. Screw on the lid and allow to stand several hours or overnight. Give the jar a shake occasionally.

Beat the cream cheese until soft. Stir in the fruit mixture to combine evenly. Spread a sheet of plastic wrap on work bench. In the centre of the sheet pile on half the mixture and spread to about 23cm long and 4cm wide to form a log. Fold the plastic wrap over the log and roll up. Smooth the log into shape and twist the ends.

Form a second log with remaining fruit/cheese mixture. Refrigerate several hours. Unroll onto a flat serving plate and serve with water crackers.

TIP

For presentation, roll the log in toasted, slivered almonds. Fruit Cheese may also be shaped into 6cm rounds.

Lemon Ginger Pears in Green Salad

INGREDIENTS

1 x 200g packet *Angas Park Pears*

¼ cup lemon juice

1 tsp ground ginger

½ tsp sugar

salt and freshly ground black pepper

500g mixed salad greens

1 cup garlic-flavoured croutons

½ cup vinaigrette dressing

Place the pears in a flat, non-metal dish in one layer. Mix together the lemon juice, ginger, sugar, salt and pepper and pour over the pears. Cover and stand 3 hours or more to absorb flavours (may be left overnight).

To crisp the salad greens, rinse in a colander under running water, drain well, shake dry in a clean tea towel and place in the refrigerator wrapped in the damp towel. Cut pears in half lengthwise and toss with salad greens. Add croutons and vinaigrette dressing. Toss well and serve.

Lemon Ginger Pears may be stored, covered, in the refrigerator for several days. They also complement the flavour of chicken, seafood and avocado.

TIP

To hasten the marinating process, place pears in the microwave for 1 minute on high and then stand 1 hour.

Glazed Pears and Parsnips

INGREDIENTS

3 medium-sized parsnips

3 *Angas Park Pears*

1 tbsp butter

1 tbsp honey

1 tsp ground ginger

salt and freshly ground black pepper

Peel parsnips, then cut into 3 even lengths. Cut into julienne-like strips, avoiding the centre core in the upper section. Cut pears into 5cm-wide strips.

Heat butter in a frying pan, add parsnip strips and sauté gently until just soft. Use an egg slice to toss them over in the butter. Add pear strips and sauté a little longer. Add the honey, ginger, salt and pepper. Gently toss the pears and parsnips in the honey glaze to coat well. Remove to a warm serving dish. Serve with grilled chicken, pork or lamb.

Brandied Dried Fruits

INGREDIENTS

1½ cups water

¾ cup sugar

zest of 1 lemon peeled off in long thin strips

2cm piece fresh ginger root, peeled

150g (1 cup) *Angas Park Diced Apricots*

1 x 200g packet *Angas Park Peaches*, cut into 6 pieces

Place the water, sugar, lemon zest and ginger into a saucepan. Bring to the boil, stirring until sugar dissolves. Boil gently for 5 minutes.

Place all dried fruits into a glass bowl. Pour over the boiling liquid and add the cinnamon stick. Stand, covered, until cold.

Remove the lemon zest and cinnamon stick. Stir in the brandy and liqueur. Spoon into jars and seal tightly. Leave to mature for 2 weeks before using. Store in a cool place, or in the refrigerator in hot weather. Serve with vanilla ice cream.

INGREDIENTS CONT.

75g (½ cup) *Angas Park Seeded Raisins*, roughly chopped

75g (½ cup) *Angas Park Sultanas*

½ cinnamon stick

¾ cup brandy

2 tbsp fruit-based liqueur

School Lunch Box Sandwich Fillings

Cheese and Raisin

Combine 200g grated cheddar cheese and 2 tablespoons of *Angas Park Raisins* moistened with a little mayonnaise.

Fruity Turkey

Mix 2 chopped turkey slices with 1 tablespoon *Angas Park Fruit Medley* and 1 tablespoon mayonnaise.

Sultana and Peanut Butter

Spread a slice of bread with peanut butter and sprinkle with *Angas Park Sultanas*.

Egg and Apricot

Mix mashed, hard-boiled egg with salt, pepper, mayonnaise and 1 tablespoon of *Angas Park Diced Apricots*. Spread on sandwich bread and top with shredded lettuce.

After-school Snacks

Apricot Mini-sandwich

Angas Park Fancy Large Apricots sandwiched together with:

cream cheese

or

peanut butter

or

ricotta cheese.

Fruit Yoghurt

200ml of plain yoghurt mixed with:

1 tablespoon of *Angas Park Fruit Medley* and 1 teaspoon of honey

or

1 tablespoon of *Angas Park Diced Apricots* and chopped walnuts.

SAO Snacks

SAO Biscuits spread with:

ricotta cheese and *Angas Park Apricots*

or

cottage cheese mixed with *Angas Park Fruit Medley* and honey.

Something to Start

The tangy taste of Angas Park dried fruits is an ideal start to any party or meal. This chapter includes a selection of savouries, canapés, hors d'oeuvres, soups and entrées to start formal dinners and informal parties, or to accompany drinks with a few friends.

Photographed from left, clockwise: Brandied Prune Pinwheels, recipe page 18; Apricot Canapés, recipe page 18; Ham and Cheese Savouries, recipe page 18.

17

Apricot Canapés

INGREDIENTS

250g cream cheese

½ cup mayonnaise

½ cup chopped walnuts

Mix together the cream cheese and mayonnaise until soft and fluffy. Add the walnuts and sherry, mix to combine. Place a teaspoonful onto each dried apricot half, arrange on a platter. Serve at room temperature. Other topping combinations include cream cheese with chopped ham and mayonnaise, or cream cheese with chopped gherkin and Tabasco sauce.

Makes 25-30

INGREDIENTS CONT.

2 tsp sherry (optional)

1 x 200g packet *Angas Park Large Apricots*

Ham and Cheese Savouries

INGREDIENTS

250g cream cheese

½ cup plain yoghurt

¾ cup (125g) *Angas Park Diced Apricots*

Soften the cream cheese by creaming with a wooden spoon. Stir in the yoghurt. In a separate bowl, combine the apricots, raisins and ham, mix evenly, then stir into the cream cheese. Refrigerate for 1 hour. Heap a generous amount onto each cracker, stand at room temperature 10 minutes before serving.

Makes 25-30

INGREDIENTS CONT.

2 tbsp (50g) *Angas Park Seeded Raisins*, chopped

200g shaved ham, finely chopped

1 packet water crackers

Brandied Prune Pinwheels

INGREDIENTS

8 large *Angas Park Prunes*

1 tbsp brandy

100g ricotta cheese

1 tsp ground cinnamon

8 slices square-cut chicken loaf or thinly-sliced sandwich ham

Remove pit from the prunes. Finely chop on a chopping board with a large knife. Work knife back and forth until prunes are almost pulverised. Place in a bowl and add the brandy. Stand 10 minutes.

Mix the ricotta cheese and cinnamon into the prunes. Spread a heaped teaspoonful onto the chicken loaf or ham slices, spreading right to the edges. Roll up and place, seam side down, on a plate, cover and refrigerate 1 hour. Cut into 4 or 5 pieces and serve, cut side up, to show pinwheel effect.

Makes 35 pieces

TIP

A combination of chicken loaf and ham pinwheels makes an attractive platter.

Pear Vichyssoise

INGREDIENTS

1 x 200g packet *Angas Park Pears*

1 tbsp butter

1 leek, white part only, thinly sliced

1 small Spanish onion, thinly sliced

1 medium potato, peeled and sliced

5 cups water

2 level tbsp chicken stock powder

300ml thickened cream

2cm piece fresh ginger root (for *Fresh Ginger Juice*)

¼ tsp nutmeg

sprigs of watercress, for garnish

Reserve 2 pear halves for the garnish and roughly dice the remainder. Melt the butter in a saucepan, add the leek and onion and stir to coat with the butter. Turn down the heat to very low, cover with a lid and allow to sweat until soft but not coloured (about 10 minutes).

Add the potato, diced pears, water and chicken stock powder. Bring to the boil, then turn down the heat and simmer for 30 minutes. Cool the soup slightly and purée in a blender or food processor, or rub through a sieve. Place in a glass or stainless steel bowl.

Stir the cream into the soup and add 1-2 teaspoons of fresh ginger juice (see Tip) and the nutmeg. If the soup is too thick, add a little milk or stock. Cover with plastic wrap and place in the refrigerator for several hours to chill—for best results, stand the bowl of soup in a basin of ice cubes in the refrigerator.

Finely dice the reserved pears. Garnish with a sprinkling of diced pear and a sprig of watercress.

TIP

Fresh Ginger Juice: peel a 2cm piece of fresh ginger root, cut it into ½ cm cubes and press the juice with a garlic crusher into a small bowl.

Alternatively, grate a peeled piece of ginger with a fine grater onto a plate, then tilt the plate to let the juice run while pressing the fibre with the back of a spoon.

Spiced Apricot Meat Balls with Apricot Dipping Sauce

INGREDIENTS

Meat Balls

¾ cup *Angas Park Diced Apricots*

2 tbsp brandy

500g prime minced beef

1 medium onion, very finely chopped

1 slice white bread, crusts removed and soaked in ¼ cup water

½ tsp ground cinnamon

pinch of ground nutmeg

1 tsp salt

½ tsp pepper

1 egg

oil for frying

Apricot Dipping Sauce

½ cup *Angas Park Diced Apricots*

1 cup water

2 tsp sugar

2 tsp balsamic vinegar

1 tsp teriyaki sauce

1 tsp fresh ginger juice (see Tip on page 19)

Meat Balls

Soak the diced apricots in the brandy for 1 hour.

In a large bowl, combine the mince with the remaining meat ball ingredients except the oil. Knead well with hand for 2 minutes to distribute ingredients evenly and to make a fine-textured mixture. Cover and refrigerate 1 hour to allow flavours to blend.

Take a heaped teaspoon of mixture and roll into a ball with wet hands. Flatten slightly and press thumb in centre to form a deep depression. Place ¼ teaspoon of soaked apricots in centre and remould into a ball, covering the apricot dice. Place on a flat tray and continue to roll the remainder. Cover with plastic wrap and refrigerate 30 minutes (or more) before frying.

Heat enough oil to be 1cm deep in a large, heavy-based frying pan or an electric frying pan set at 180°C. Fry meat balls in 2 or 3 batches, rolling them around the pan to cook all over and keep their shape.

Drain on kitchen paper. Place on a heated serving platter, with dipping sauce in the centre and toothpicks for serving.

Apricot Dipping Sauce

Place diced apricots and water in a saucepan with any remaining brandy-soaked apricots. Bring to the boil, turn down heat and simmer 15 minutes or until very soft.

Stir in sugar, vinegar, teriyaki sauce and simmer 2 minutes. Purée in a blender or pass through a sieve. Stir in the fresh ginger juice, serve with the apricot meat balls.

Makes 20-25

Prune and Proscuitto Rolls

INGREDIENTS

150g proscuitto

250g packet *Angas Park Pitted Prunes*

toothpicks

Cut each proscuitto slice in half across the width and then in half again down its length.

Wrap a strip of proscuitto around each prune. Secure with a toothpick.

Serve as an hors d'oeuvre.

Makes 24

Apricot and Sausage Kebabs

INGREDIENTS

4 pork sausages

125g *Angas Park Apricots*

1 tbsp honey

2 tsp soy sauce

1 tsp water

Prick sausages and cook carefully under a grill or on a grill plate or frying pan. Turn frequently to cook evenly. Allow to cool.

Cut into 1 or $1^{1}/_{2}$ cm-thick slices. Thread sausage round onto a cocktail stick and place apricot half at each end.

Mix honey, soy sauce and water together. Brush over kebabs, place under a hot grill until well glazed, or place in a moderate oven for 10 minutes. Serve hot as finger food.

Makes approximately 16

Dolmades

INGREDIENTS

500g preserved vine
leaves

¾ cup olive oil

2 large onions, very
finely chopped

1 cup short grain rice

3 tbsp pine nuts

3 tbsp finely chopped
parsley

2 tsp chopped mint

3 tbsp *Angas Park
Currants*

1 cup hot water

1 tsp salt

½ tsp pepper

juice of 1 lemon

1¼ cups hot water, extra

Rinse vine leaves in cold water. Have a large pot of boiling water and a large bowl of cold water ready. Drop about one quarter of the leaves into the boiling water for 2 minutes, then lift out with tongs and place in the cold water. Repeat with remainder. Drain well.

Heat half the oil in a saucepan and lightly fry the onion. Add rice and pine nuts and stir over heat for a minute or until coloured. Add parsley, mint, currants, 1 cup of hot water, salt and pepper. Cover tightly and simmer for 10 minutes, until water is absorbed. Turn off heat and stand 10 minutes, covered.

Place a vine leaf, shiny side down and stem end towards you, on work surface, snip off the stem, if any. Put a heaped teaspoon of stuffing in centre. Fold stem end and sides over stuffing and roll up, not too tight. Repeat with the remainder.

Line a large, heavy-based saucepan or lidded skillet with a few vine leaves and pack rolls in, close together, seam side down. Pour over remaining olive oil, lemon juice and the extra hot water. Invert a suitably-sized plate over top to keep the rolls in shape while cooking. Bring to boil, place on lid, turn down heat and simmer 1 hour. Add water during cooking if needed. When cooked, turn off heat and allow to cool in the juices for 1 hour.

Lift onto serving platter. Chill before serving. Garnish with lemon slices. Serve as an appetiser or entrée.

Makes approximately 50

Chilled Fruit Soup

INGREDIENTS

200g *Angas Park Pears*

200g *Angas Park Apricots*

200g *Angas Park Peaches*

4 cups water

¼ cup sugar

1 whole clove

1 cinnamon stick

grated zest and juice of 1 lemon

Reserve one piece of each fruit for garnish. Place remainder in a saucepan, add the water and soak for 10 minutes. Add remaining ingredients. Bring to the boil, then turn down the heat and simmer slowly for 20 minutes, until fruit is tender. Remove cinnamon stick and clove.

Purée fruit and liquid in a blender, or rub fruit through a sieve, adding liquid to make a fairly thick consistency. Chill soup well for several hours.

Chop the reserved dried fruits. Serve soup in chilled bowls, garnish with a sprinkling of chopped fruits.

Serves 6

Pear and Pork Pâté

INGREDIENTS

500g pork mince

5 rashers bacon, finely chopped

500g chicken thigh fillets, diced

2 cloves garlic, crushed

15 black peppercorns

15 juniper berries

150ml chicken stock

2 tbsp brandy

lard or bacon fat, for greasing

1 x 200g packet *Angas Park Pears*

Mix pork mince, chopped bacon and diced chicken thigh fillets together, add garlic, peppercorns and juniper berries. Mix well with hand to evenly distribute all ingredients. Stir in the chicken stock and brandy, and combine well.

Grease a pâté mould or an 11 x 24cm loaf tin with bacon fat or lard. Line the base with a piece of foil cut to fit. Grease up surface of foil. Place 3 or 4 dried pear halves, smooth side down, along the centre of the pâté mould or loaf tin. Pour in half of the pork mixture. Cover surface with remaining dried pears and pour in the remaining pork mixture. Place lid on mould or cover pan with foil.

Stand in a baking dish with hot water to come half way up the side of the mould. Cook in preheated oven 180°C for $1^1/_2$ hours or until it has shrunk away from the sides slightly.

When cooked, remove from oven and allow to stand for 20 minutes. Remove lid or foil. Cover surface with greased paper then place a weight on top, up to $1^1/_2$ kg. This can be achieved by placing another loaf tin or other platform to rest inside the edges of the dish and then placing heavy weights (e.g. cans of food etc.) on top. Distribute the weight evenly and stand for several hours, until the pâté is cold. Remove the weights and refrigerate.

To unmould, run a round-bladed knife around sides, overturn on flat serving plate, shake once and remove mould. Carefully remove foil. Slice and serve with salad garnish. Serve as an entrée or luncheon dish.

Serves 10-12

Peach and Prawn Entrée Salad

INGREDIENTS

1 x 200g packet *Angas Park Peaches*

1 tbsp lemon juice

2 tsp grated lemon zest

2 tsp brown sugar

½ tsp salt

½ tsp freshly ground black pepper

⅓ cup sherry vinegar

2 drops Tabasco sauce

500g mesclun salad mix

2 tsp Dijon mustard

INGREDIENTS CONT.

1 egg

⅔ cup light olive oil

12 king prawns, shelled and deveined

Place dried peaches in a flat, non-metal dish. Mix the next 7 ingredients together and pour over the peaches. Cover and stand at room temperature for 30 minutes. Rinse mesclun salad mix in a colander under running water. Drain well, shake dry in a clean tea towel, then place in the refrigerator wrapped in the damp towel to crisp.

Remove peaches from the vinegar mixture. Pour the vinegar mixture into a blender or food processor, add the mustard and egg, and process until smooth. With the motor running, add the oil in a thin, steady stream; dressing will become creamy and thicken slightly.

Divide salad mix between 4 plates, piling high in centre of plate. Place 2 peach halves on slope of salad and arrange 3 prawns on each plate. Spoon dressing over the salad and serve immediately.

Serves 4

Pear and Pepperleaf Soup

INGREDIENTS

2 tbsp oil

⅓ cup macadamia nuts,
roughly chopped

1 leek, white part only,
washed and thinly sliced

1 medium-sized onion,
roughly chopped

1 x 200g packet *Angas
Park Pears*

1 litre chicken stock

1½ tsp ground pepperleaf

½ tsp salt

¾ cup cream

In a small pan heat 2 teaspoons of the oil, add the macadamia nuts and stir to lightly roast to a pale colour. Remove and drain on kitchen paper.

In a large saucepan heat remaining oil, add leek and onion and sauté gently for 2 minutes, until soft but not coloured. Add pears, chicken stock, pepperleaf and salt. Bring to the boil, then turn down heat and simmer for 15 minutes. Cool slightly then purée in a blender or food processor. Return to saucepan. Add cream and reheat over low heat, stirring occasionally.

Serve in soup bowls and garnish with a sprinkling of toasted macadamia nuts.

Serves 6-8

Salami Stacks

INGREDIENTS

250g cream cheese

½ cup (80g) *Angas Park Diced Apricots*

4 tbsp mayonnaise

½ tsp Tabasco sauce

16 slices Danish salami

¾ cup extra *Angas Park Diced Apricots*, finely chopped

Bring cream cheese to room temperature, cream well to soften. Reserve 3 tablespoons of cream cheese, leave at room temperature. Stir the diced apricots, mayonnaise and Tabasco into the bowl of cream cheese.

Spread a heaped teaspoon of cheese mixture on a salami slice, making sure it is spread right to the edge. Place second salami slice on top and spread as above. Repeat with one more slice and top with the fourth slice. Repeat with remaining ingredients to make 4 stacks of 4 slices of salami. Place on a flat plate, cover with plastic wrap and refrigerate for 2 hours.

Take the extra ¾ cup diced apricots and chop very finely. Spread on kitchen paper in a 1½ cm-wide strip. Lightly spread reserved cream cheese around sides of stacks. Roll the sides over the chopped apricots, press on well. Cover and refrigerate. To serve, cut each stack into 6 triangles. Place a toothpick in centre of each and arrange on platter.

Makes 24

TIP

To ensure easy spreading, keep the reserved 3 tbsp of cream cheese at room temperature until needed.

Something New

New ideas and new flavour combinations are made possible with the wider use of Angas Park dried fruits—they will change the tone of family meals and delight your dinner guests. A quick, pan-fried steak becomes a gourmet meal with the simple addition of sautéed dried fruit. Create your own recipes by interchanging the dried fruits and other ingredients suggested in this chapter.

Photographed from left: Pork fillets with Prunes in Sherry Sauce, recipe page 32; Sweet Lamb Chop Curry, recipe page 33.

31

Pork Fillets with Prunes in Sherry Sauce

INGREDIENTS

125g (approx. 20) *Angas Park Pitted Prunes*

150ml (over ½ cup) sherry

2 pork long fillets (approx. 400g each)

salt and freshly ground pepper

½ bunch fresh chives, washed and dried

2 tbsp butter

¼ cup water

1 tbsp flour

150ml cream

2 tbsp red currant jelly

Soak prunes in the sherry for several hours or overnight.

Trim pork fillets, removing fine connective tissue from surface and stripping off the thicker, shiny, white layer with a sharp knife.

With a large, sharp knife, make a deep slit in each fillet along the side of the length, to within 1cm of the other side, leaving fillet still attached. Open out and lightly flatten with the side of a meat mallet. Season with salt and pepper.

Drain the prunes, reserve the sherry marinade. Split the prunes open and lay along the fillet. Lay several chives over the prunes to cover all the length. Fold the fillet back into position and tie at 2cm intervals with kitchen string.

Heat butter in a large frying pan, add fillets and brown quickly on all sides. Remove to a baking dish. Sprinkle with a little salt and pepper. Pour over the sherry marinade and add the water to the dish. Cook in a preheated oven 180°C for 1 hour. Place on a hot serving platter and remove the string. Cover with foil.

Place baking dish over moderate hot plate. Add flour and stir into the juices until free of lumps. Add a little water if necessary to dissolve or wash down any browned-on juices. When simmering, stir in the cream and red currant jelly. Pour into a sauce boat.

Slice the pork fillets thickly and serve, cut side up, with the sherry sauce and vegetable accompaniments.

Serves 4-6

Sweet Lamb Chop Curry

INGREDIENTS

6 forequarter lamb chops
(approx. 850g)

1 tbsp oil

1 large onion, finely
chopped

1 clove garlic, crushed

1½ tbsp Madras-style
curry powder

½ tsp ground ginger

2 cups water

salt and pepper

¾ cup *Angas Park Fruit
Medley*

1 tsp brown sugar

½ cinnamon stick

½ cup plain yoghurt
(optional)

Trim excess fat from the chops. Wipe over with kitchen paper.

Heat oil in a large, heavy-based saucepan or lidded skillet. Add onion and garlic and fry until golden over moderate heat. Remove onion with a slotted spoon, set aside.

Increase heat, and brown chops quickly on both sides. Do only 2 or 3 at a time. Remove to plate and drain almost all fat from the pan.

Add the curry powder and ginger to the hot saucepan and stir over heat to roast until aroma rises. Stir in the water, lifting the pan juices as you stir. Season with salt and pepper.

Return lamb and onion, cover and simmer for 1 hour.

Add fruit medley, brown sugar and cinnamon stick and simmer for approximately 1 hour, until lamb is very soft and tender. Add more water during cooking if necessary.

Remove chops to a hot serving platter. Stir yoghurt into the sauce (if desired) and pour sauce over the chops. Serve with boiled rice.

Serves 4-6

Marinated Chicken and Pear Salad

INGREDIENTS

1 large barbecued chicken

1 x 200g packet *Angas Park Pears*

Marinade

½ cup olive oil

¼ cup orange juice

2 tbsp red wine vinegar

3 whole cloves

3 whole bay leaves

2 tbsp pine nuts

¼ cup *Angas Park Seeded Raisins*

INGREDIENTS CONT.

salt and pepper, to taste

½ tsp finely chopped red chilli

Salad

1 coral lettuce

1 mignonette lettuce

1 bunch roquette

2 Lebanese cucumbers, thinly sliced

1 small Spanish onion, thinly sliced

Cut chicken and separate the breast and legs. Remove bones and cut into wide strips. Place neatly into a flat-based, non-metal container. Place pear halves over the chicken.

Combine marinade ingredients in a bowl, whisk well and pour over chicken. Cover and refrigerate for 2 hours or more. Turn chicken and pears after 1 hour so top pieces sit in marinade.

To crisp the lettuce leaves, rinse in a colander under running water, drain well, shake dry in a clean tea towel and place in the refrigerator wrapped in the damp towel. Toss together the prepared salad vegetables. Pile onto a suitable platter. Arrange chicken strips and pear halves over salad. Spoon over the raisins and pine nuts.

Whisk the remaining marinade again, adding a little extra oil and vinegar if needed. Pour over the salad. Serve immediately.

Serves 8

Chicken Rolls with Orange Currant Sauce

INGREDIENTS

2 tsp grated orange zest

4 strips thinly peeled orange zest, cut into thin strips (julienne)

juice of 3 oranges

1 small onion, finely chopped and fried in a little butter

¼ cup fresh breadcrumbs

2 tbsp (30g) *Angas Park Currants*

1kg chicken thigh fillets

salt and pepper

2 ginger nut biscuits, finely crushed

2 tbsp brandy

Mix together grated orange zest, 2 tablespoons of the orange juice, fried onions and breadcrumbs. Flatten chiken thigh fillets with a meat mallet, smooth side down, and sprinkle with salt and pepper. Place a teaspoon of filling onto each fillet, pressing on well. Roll up and secure with a toothpick.

Heat butter or oil in a heavy-based frying pan and brown on all sides. Reduce heat and add remaining orange juice, scraping up any browned juices with the back of a spoon. Add currants and a pinch of salt and pepper. Cover and simmer for 20 minutes, until chicken rolls are tender. Remove rolls to a warm serving platter, keep hot.

To the pan juices add the crushed ginger nut biscuits. Stir over low heat until thickened. If a thinner consistency is desired add extra orange juice or water. Pour over chicken rolls and garnish with blanched julienne orange zest.

Serves 6

TIP

To blanch julienne orange zest, place in a saucepan with a little water and bring to the boil. Drain and add cold water. Remove and pat dry.

Pear and Ginger Chicken Parcels

INGREDIENTS

4 chicken breast fillets

salt and pepper

1 tbsp butter or oil

2 tbsp water

4 *Angas Park Pears*

8 sheets filo pastry

½ cup melted butter

1 small jar preserved ginger in syrup

2 tbsp flaked almonds

Place chicken fillets between 2 sheets of plastic wrap and flatten with a meat mallet to even the thickness. Sprinkle with salt and pepper. Place in a hot pan with butter and brown on each side, but do not cook through. Remove chicken fillets and stir in the water.

Place in pear halves and simmer for a few minutes to absorb pan juices and water, turning over as they cook. Remove and cool.

Brush a sheet of filo pastry with melted butter and place a second sheet on top, brush with butter. Fold in half and brush top.

Trim chicken fillet, slit in half. Place one half in centre of pastry square towards the front. Top with a pear half and a little preserved ginger and syrup. Top with remaining chicken half. Fold front piece of pastry over chicken, fold in the sides then turn over to form a parcel. Repeat with remainder of ingredients.

Place parcels, seam side down, on a greased baking tray, brush with melted butter and sprinkle with flaked almonds. Place in preheated oven 180° C and bake for 20 minutes. Serve with vegetable accompaniments.

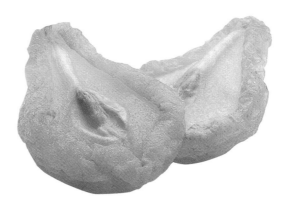

Chicken and Pear Curry

INGREDIENTS

5 *Angas Park Pears*

1 tbsp butter

1 tbsp oil

500g chicken tenderloin
or stir fry

1 medium onion, finely
chopped

1 tbsp Madras-style curry
powder

1 tsp sugar

INGREDIENTS CONT.

½ cup cream

½ cup white wine

2 tbsp shredded coconut

2 tbsp toasted cashew
nuts

Cut pears into 1cm strips, set aside. Heat butter and oil in a large frying pan, add chicken and brown on both sides to seal. Remove from pan.

Add onion and fry gently until soft. Stir in curry powder and cook 1 minute. Reduce heat. Add sugar, cream, wine and coconut, stir well.

Return chicken to pan and add pears. Cover and simmer 15 minutes, taking care not to boil.

Remove to a heated dish and sprinkle with toasted cashew nuts. Serve with boiled rice.

Serves 4

Apricot Chicken Roulade

INGREDIENTS

Chicken Roulade

1kg chicken mince

1 cup soft breadcrumbs

1 clove garlic, crushed

1 tsp salt

¼ tsp pepper

2 tbsp lemon juice

1 tbsp water

2 tbsp chopped parsley

Filling

120g *Angas Park Apricots*

¾ cup water

1 tsp sugar

1 small onion, finely chopped

½ cup diced celery

1 cup soft breadcrumbs

Glaze

2 tbsp apricot purée (reserved from filling)

2 tsp sugar

2 tsp teriyaki sauce

Roulade

Mix all the ingredients for the roulade together, kneading well with hand. Set aside and make the filling (see below).

Place a 35cm length of plastic wrap on work bench. Spread over the mince mixture to form a rectangle approximately 28 x 23cm. Spread the apricot filling over the mince.

To make a roll, hold the plastic wrap towards the front and lift high, leaning towards the back until about 4cm of the mince folds over on itself. Continue pulling towards the back, forming a roll as you pull.

Roll onto a greased oven slide and remove plastic wrap. Pat the roll into shape. Press the 5 apricots reserved from the filling along the top. Brush with glaze (see below) and place in a preheated oven 180°C for 40 minutes. Brush with glaze several times during cooking.

Serve hot with vegetables or cold with salad.

Filling

Reserve 5 apricots for garnish. Place remainder in a saucepan with water and sugar. Cover and cook until apricots are soft. Uncover to allow most of the water to evaporate, stirring well to form a purée. Reserve 2 tablespoons of the purée for the glaze. Mix remaining filling ingredients into the rest of the purée.

Glaze

To make the glaze, simply mix the glaze ingredients together.

Serves 6

Beef and Pears Stroganoff-style

INGREDIENTS

1 x 200g packet *Angas Park Pears*

1 tbsp flour

½ tsp salt

500g beef stir fry

1½ tbsp butter

1½ tbsp oil

1 large onion, thinly sliced

1 clove garlic

1 tsp brown sugar

2 tsp flour, extra

1½ cups beef stock

2 tsp fresh ginger juice (see Tip on page 19)

salt to taste

freshly ground black pepper

1 tbsp balsamic vinegar

150ml sour cream

2 tbsp chopped parsley

Cut pears into 5cm strips and set aside.

Mix flour and salt together. Pat the beef strips dry with kitchen paper, place in a plastic bag and add the flour, shake well to coat.

Heat a large heavy-based pan to hot over high heat, add butter and oil, swirl to cover base then add the beef strips and brown rapidly on all sides. The strips should remain very juicy and pink on the inside. Remove from the pan and keep hot.

Reduce heat, add onion, garlic and a little extra oil if needed. Sprinkle brown sugar over onion and cook until onion is soft and golden.

Sprinkle the 2 teaspoons of flour over the onion, stirring in well. Gradually add the stock and stir to lift up the pan juices. Simmer 2 minutes.

Return meat strips and any juices back to the pan, add ginger juice and season with salt and pepper. Simmer for 10 minutes.

Add pear strips, toss in well and simmer for 5 minutes. Add balsamic vinegar and stir in sour cream. Heat through on low heat. Pour into hot serving dish and sprinkle with parsley. Serve with boiled rice or noodles.

Serves 4-5

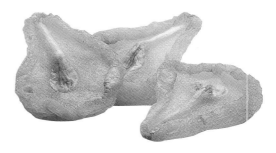

Hot Beef and Peach Salad with Herb Dressing

INGREDIENTS

300g mesclun salad mix

2 boneless sirloin steaks, 1½ cm thick

salt and freshly ground black pepper

2 tsp olive oil

1 tbsp brandy

2 tsp butter

2 tbsp finely chopped shallots

6 *Angas Park Peaches*

Herb Dressing

1 tbsp chopped chives

1 tbsp chopped parsley

2 tsp green peppercorns

1 tsp Dijon mustard

½ cup tarragon vinegar

½ cup olive oil

salt and pepper

Before cooking the steaks, crisp the salad (see Tip).

Remove steaks from refrigerator, wipe dry with kitchen paper and sprinkle with freshly ground pepper. Allow to come to room temperature (about 20 minutes).

Prepare salad dressing by mixing all salad dressing ingredients together in a screw-top jar, shake well. Season steaks with salt and more pepper.

Heat a large, heavy-based frying pan on high heat until a drop of water splashed in the pan sizzles and bounces on contact. Add oil and swirl to coat pan. Place in the steaks and sear over high heat for 45 seconds on each side. Pour in the brandy, ignite with a taper and remove the pan from heat until flames die down. Remove steaks to a heated plate and keep hot.

Add butter to pan and add shallots and peaches. Sauté a little, turning peaches over. Remove peaches and pour juices and shallots over steaks.

With a sharp knife, slice the steaks thinly on the diagonal and arrange, with peaches, around and on the salad. Pour over any juices. Reshake dressing and spoon over the salad and meat. Serve immediately with hot, crusty bread.

Serves 4

TIP

To crisp the lettuce leaves, rinse in a colander under running water, drain well, shake dry in a clean tea towel and place in the refrigerator wrapped in the damp towel.

Veal and Peach Melts

INGREDIENTS

4 large, thinly-sliced veal
steaks

1 tbsp butter

1 tbsp oil

salt and freshly ground
pepper

½ cup white onions,
chopped

1 x 200g packet *Angas
Park Peaches*

4 slices pre-sliced Swiss
cheese

If steaks are not even thickness, pound a little to even out. Heat a large heavy-based frying pan, add half the butter and oil and swirl to cover base. Quickly add 2 steaks and cook very quickly to brown on each side. Sprinkle with salt and pepper as they cook. Remove to a plate, keep hot and cook remaining steaks, adding remaining butter and oil if needed. Remove. Reduce heat and add white onions, sauté a little then add peaches, sauté a little on each side.

Cut steaks in half. Place half of each steak on oven tray and stack with peach, shallots, other steak half, peach and top with a Swiss cheese slice.

Place tray in a preheated hot oven until cheese melts and encases the stack (about 1½ minutes). Alternatively, it may be placed under a hot griller. Serve immediately with vegetable accompaniments.

Serves 4

Ham Steaks with Fruity Sauce

INGREDIENTS

Fruity Sauce

½ cup *Angas Park Fruit Medley*

1½ cups water

½ tsp salt

2 tbsp brown sugar

1 tsp Worcestershire sauce

3-4 drops Tabasco sauce

Fruity Sauce

Place the fruit medley in a saucepan, add the water and soak for ½ hour. Add remaining sauce ingredients except the cornflour and bring to the boil, turn down and simmer, covered, for 20 minutes. Add blended cornflour and stir until sauce thickens.

Ham Steaks

Heat butter in a frying pan and fry ham steaks on both sides until rosy brown. Serve with Fruity Sauce and vegetable accompaniments. This dish is also delicious with Raisin Sauce (page 88).

Serves 3-4

INGREDIENTS CONT.

2 tbsp brown sugar

1 tbsp cornflour, blended with a little water

Ham Steaks

6 ham steaks

butter for frying

Baked Pumpkin and Pears

INGREDIENTS

400g butternut or Jap
pumpkin

1 x 200g packet *Angas
Park Pears*

⅓ cup water

½ tsp salt

freshly ground black
pepper

2 tsp brown sugar

1 tbsp butter

Cut pumpkin into 1cm slices, trim off skin. Place in a shallow, rectangular, ovenprooof dish, overlapping alternately with the pears. Drizzle in the water, making sure all surface area is moistened. Sprinkle with salt, pepper and brown sugar. Dot the butter over the surface. Cover with foil, sealing around the edges. Place in a preheated moderate oven and cook 20 minutes.

Remove foil and return dish to the oven, uncovered, continue cooking for 5 to 10 minutes, until caramelised on top. Serve hot as an accompaniment to grilled meats or chicken.

Serves 4-6

Apricot-studded Baked Ham

INGREDIENTS

1 x 4kg leg of ham

2 tbsp butter

2 tbsp brown sugar

2 tbsp powdered mustard

3 tbsp flour

½ cup water

Glaze

1 x 200g packet *Angas Park Fancy Large Apricots*

1 cup water

½ cup brown sugar

1 tsp ground ginger

1 tsp brown or cider vinegar

Remove rind from the ham and carefully trim off fat, leaving only a thin layer covering the ham.

Initial Baking

Melt butter in a saucepan, add 2 tablespoons brown sugar and stir well, then add mustard and flour, mix well. Remove from heat, add the ½ cup of water, a little at a time, to make a smooth paste. Stir over heat until it bubbles.

Place the ham in a baking dish and spread the paste over the fat surface. Place in a hot oven 220°C for 20 minutes, until paste has set, then turn down to 180°C and bake 30 minutes more. Remove from oven.

Glaze

Place apricots in a saucepan, add the cup of water and stir in ½ cup brown sugar. Bring to the boil, then simmer for 5 minutes. Remove apricots from liquid with a slotted spoon and set aside.

To the liquid in the saucepan add the ginger and vinegar. Boil until reduced by half and liquid has become a slightly thickened syrup/glaze (take care not to reduce to toffee stage).

Final Baking

Stud the surface of the ham with the apricots. Secure each apricot with a toothpick to keep in place and brush well with the glaze. Return to oven and continue cooking for 20 minutes, brushing every 5 minutes with glaze. Remove toothpicks—the apricots will now remain in place, brush with glaze and cook 2-5 minutes more. Transfer to serving platter and attach a frill on shank end.

TIP

To serve a cold decorated ham, the Initial Baking can be omitted–simply place the apricots onto the trimmed ham, glaze and bake, as directed in Final Baking.

Braised Rabbit with Dried Fruits

INGREDIENTS

1½ kg rabbit

salt and pepper

2 tbsp oil or clarified butter

6 small onions, halved

2 cups water

1 tbsp chopped, fresh thyme

2 bay leaves

1 x 200g packet *Angas Park Fruit Salad*

150ml red wine

150ml cream

Wash rabbit and pat dry. Cut into serving pieces. Season with salt and pepper. Heat oil or butter in a large, lidded frying pan or saucepan. Add rabbit pieces and quickly brown all sides on high heat.

Remove to a plate. Reduce heat, add onions and cook until golden. Add water and stir to lift pan juices. Return rabbit to the pan, sprinkle in the chopped thyme and add bay leaves. Cover and simmer for 40 minutes.

Add the fruit salad and wine, cover and continue to simmer for 30 minutes more, or until rabbit is tender. Add more liquid to saucepan during cooking if necessary. Taste and adjust seasoning. Uncover and stir in the cream. Simmer with lid off for 5 minutes. Serve with rice or mashed potato.

Serves 6

Roast Chicken with Apricot and Raisin Stuffing

INGREDIENTS

Apricot and Raisin Stuffing

100g *Angas Park Diced Apricots*

100g *Angas Park Seeded Raisins*, chopped

2 tbsp butter

1 medium onion, finely chopped

2½ cups white breadcrumbs

¼ tsp mixed spice

salt and pepper

1 egg, beaten

Chicken

1 size 18 fresh chicken

½ lemon

salt and pepper

1 cup water

1 medium onion, quartered

1 carrot, thickly sliced

¼ cup water, extra

1 tbsp flour blended with 2 tbsp water

Apricot and Raisin Stuffing

Soak apricots and raisins in cold water to cover for 1 hour or in hot water for 30 minutes.

Heat butter in a small pan and lightly fry onion until pale golden colour. Drain apricots and raisins well, place in a bowl and mix in onion, remaining melted butter and all other stuffing ingredients.

Chicken

Wash chicken well, taking care to scrape out cavity with a fork. Rinse cavity well under running water. Drain then pat dry, inside and out, with kitchen paper.

Rub over, inside and out, with the cut lemon half, squeezing out a little juice as you rub. Season with salt and pepper. Fill cavity with the apricot stuffing and truss the chicken, or just tie the legs together with cotton string.

Place in a roasting dish with 1 cup water, onion and carrot, which will flavour the gravy. Add a little extra water to the dish if needed during cooking. Roast for 1½ hours in a preheated oven set at 180°C. Remove chicken to a heated platter, cover with foil to keep hot.

Skim fat from pan. Add ¼ cup water, wash down any cooked-on juices, including the brown bits up the sides of the dish. Strain into a small saucepan and add the blended flour. Stir over heat until it thickens and boils. Turn down heat to very low and keep at a simmer while carving the chicken. Remove stuffing to a heated dish. Carve chicken and serve with apricot stuffing, gravy and vegetables.

Serves 6-8

TIP

When roasting a chicken always have a little water in the base of the pan to protect the chicken juices from charring, as they are needed to make a tasty gravy. As the water evaporates, and the juices become a deep rosy brown colour, add a little extra water to prevent them going black.

Veal Schnitzel with Glazed Apricots

INGREDIENTS

4 veal steaks, thinly cut

½ cup flour, seasoned
with salt and pepper

2 eggs, lightly beaten

1 cup dry breadcrumbs

1 tbsp butter

1 tbsp oil

Glazed Apricots

16 *Angas Park Apricots*

1 cup water

½ cup brown sugar

1 tsp ground ginger

4cm strip lemon zest

2 tbsp lemon juice

Pound steaks out thinly between 2 sheets plastic wrap. Dip in seasoned flour, then dip in egg to coat. Spread half the breadcrumbs on kitchen paper, place the steaks on top and cover with remaining crumbs. Press down well with palm of hand to firm the crumbs on. Place in a single layer on a tray. Cover and refrigerate 30 minutes or more.

Place all glazed apricot ingredients in a saucepan. Bring to the boil, turn down heat and simmer 5 minutes. Remove apricots from liquid with a slotted spoon and set aside. Boil liquid in the saucepan until reduced to a syrup.

Heat oil and butter in a large frying pan to hot. Add 2 schnitzels and cook about 2 minutes on each side, turn with tongs. Remove and cook the other 2 schnitzels. Drain on kitchen paper.

Serve on heated plates. Place 4 glazed apricots down centre of each schnitzel. Spoon syrup on top. Serve immediately with vegetable accompaniments.

Serves 4

TIP

To cut a strip of lemon zest, peel a thin strip off a lemon with a potato peeler.

Onion and Prune Tart

INGREDIENTS

2 cups plain flour

pinch of salt

180g butter

1 egg yolk

2 tbsp cold water

15 *Angas Park Fancy Medium Prunes*

¼ cup brandy

4 tbsp olive oil

500g onions, sliced into rings

salt and pepper

1 tsp brown sugar

2 rashers bacon, trimmed of fat, chopped

2 tbsp grated tasty cheese

Sift flour and salt together. Rub in the butter with fingers until it looks like fine breadcrumbs. Add combined egg yolk and water. Form into a dough with hand. Roll out between 2 sheets of plastic wrap. Line a 20cm flan tin with the pastry. Chill while preparing filling.

Cut prunes in half and soak in the brandy for 1 hour or more. Heat half the oil in a large frying pan. Add onions, stir well. Cover with lid, reduce heat and cook slowly for 30 minutes, stir at intervals. Uncover pan, increase heat and stir until golden, adding more oil if necessary. Season with salt, pepper and brown sugar. Add chopped bacon and stir to cook a little. Stir in the prunes and brandy.

Cool mixture a little, then place in the chilled pastry case. Sprinkle lightly with the grated cheese. Bake in a preheated hot oven 200°C for 20 minutes. Reduce the heat to 180°C and cook 10-15 minutes more. Serve hot with a salad accompaniment.

Serves 6

Scalloped Potatoes and Peaches

INGREDIENTS

4 medium potatoes, washed and peeled

salt and pepper, to taste

¼ teaspoon nutmeg

1 cup grated cheese

1 x 200g packet *Angas Park Peaches*

¾ cup cream or half milk/half cream

Butter a large casserole dish. Slice the potatoes thinly. Mix salt, pepper, nutmeg and cheese together. Place a layer of potatoes in base of casserole dish and sprinkle with 1 tablespoon of cheese mixture. Repeat with a second layer.

Place a layer of peaches over potatoes and continue with 2 layers of potatoes and cheese mixture and 1 layer of peaches until all ingredients are used. Finish with potato and cheese layer.

Pour in the cream. Cover with lid or foil. Place in a preheated oven 180°C and cook for approximately 1-1¼ hours, until potato is tender. Remove lid or foil for the last 15 minutes of cooking to brown the top. Serve as an accompaniment to meat, chicken or fish.

Serves 6-8

TIP

Left-overs should be refrigerated immediately. Reheat in a slow oven (170°C) until hot. Moisten with a little extra milk. Alternatively, reheat in a microwave on 50% power until hot.

Garlic Rice with Currants and Pine Nuts

INGREDIENTS

2 tbsp olive oil

1 large onion, chopped

3-4 cloves garlic, finely chopped

1½ cups long grain rice

¼ cup pine nuts

1 x 400g can tomatoes, chopped, juice reserved

½ tsp sugar

INGREDIENTS CONT.

1 tsp salt

¼ tsp black pepper

1 cup hot water

½ cup *Angas Park Currants*

2 tbsp chopped parsley

2 tbsp chopped mint

Heat oil in a large heavy-based saucepan and gently fry onion until pale golden. Add garlic and stir to cook a little. Add rice and pine nuts and stir to coat grains with oil and to colour slightly. This gives a nutty flavour.

Add chopped tomatoes plus juice from can. Season with sugar, salt and pepper, and add hot water.

Stir in all remaining ingredients and bring to the boil. Turn down heat and cook at a medium boil for 14 minutes, stirring occasionally during cooking. Turn off heat, cover tightly and stand 5 minutes before serving. Fluff with a fork and serve alone or as a side dish with main meals.

Serves 4

Something Traditional

Before the development of modern food production, many cultures around the world discovered the value of drying the excess fruit harvest to preserve it for use during the winter months. In its dried form, fruit became a new ingredient. As a result, many tasty dishes using dried fruits were created which eventually became traditional dishes of these cultures. The following chapter is an introduction to this culinary wealth.

Photographed from left: Glazed Chicken and Dried Fruit Compote, recipe page 55; Bobotie, recipe page 54.

53

Bobotie

BAKED CURRIED LAMB CASSEROLE — SOUTH AFRICA

INGREDIENTS

1kg boned leg or shoulder of lamb

4 *Angas Park Peaches*, chopped

½ cup *Angas Park Seeded Raisins*, chopped

1 slice white bread

¼ cup milk

2 tbsp butter or oil

3 large onions, finely chopped

2 tbsp Madras-style curry powder

1 tbsp brown sugar

salt and freshly ground black pepper

¼ cup lemon juice

3 eggs

¼ cup almonds

4 lemon leaves or bay leaves

¾ cup milk, extra

Trim fat from lamb and mince coarsely in a food processor or mincer.

Soak dried fruit in water for 30 minutes, drain and set aside. Soak the bread slice in ¼ cup milk.

Heat butter or oil in a large frying pan, add minced lamb and brown thoroughly, stirring and breaking up lumps with back of a wooden spoon. Remove from pan to a large bowl.

Add onions and extra oil to the pan, if needed, and fry onions until soft but not coloured. Add curry powder, sugar, salt and pepper, and stir for 1 minute. Stir in lemon juice, dissolving brown pan juices. Bring to the simmer, then pour contents of pan over the meat. Add milk-soaked bread, 1 of the eggs, peaches, raisins, and almonds. Knead with hand to combine all ingredients well.

Pack the lamb into a greased baking dish or heatproof lasagne dish and smooth the top. Tuck the lemon or bay leaves beneath the surface of the meat.

Beat the 2 remaining eggs with the extra ¾ cup milk, season lightly with salt and pepper, and pour over the surface of the mince.

Bake in a preheated slow oven 160°C for 40 minutes, until surface is browned and firm. Serve hot with boiled rice.

Serves 6-8

Glazed Chicken with Dried Fruit Compote

HOLLAND

INGREDIENTS

Dried Fruit Compote

1 x 200g packet *Angas Park Fruit Salad*

2 tbsp sugar

2cm piece cinnamon stick

2 cups water

1 tsp balsamic vinegar

2 tsp arrowroot, blended with 1 tbsp water

Glazed Chicken

4-6 chicken Maryland pieces

salt and freshly ground pepper

1 tbsp butter

1 tbsp oil

4 shallots, finely chopped

100ml dry white wine

100ml rich chicken stock

2 tsp arrowroot, blended with 1 tbsp water

Dried Fruit Compote

Place all compote ingredients, except the arrowroot, in a saucepan, bring to the boil then turn down heat and simmer 10 minutes.

Strain the fruit, discard the cinnamon stick and return the juice to the saucepan. Add the teaspoon of blended arrowroot to the saucepan and stir over the heat until liquid boils and thickens. Pour over the cooked fruit and cool slightly. Serve in individual glass bowls with the chicken.

Glazed Chicken

Wipe over chicken with kitchen paper, season with salt and pepper.

Heat butter and oil in a large, lidded skillet. When hot, add 2 pieces of chicken at a time and brown on both sides, turning with tongs. Remove and brown the remainder.

Return all chicken to the pan in one layer, turn down heat, cover with a lid and cook slowly for about 20 minutes. Turn after 10 minutes, cook through to the bone—juices should run clear when pierced with a skewer. Remove to a heated plate and keep hot. Add shallots and sauté until soft, then stir in wine and chicken stock.

Scrape up all brown juices. Add the blended arrowroot and stir until it boils and thickens. Simmer a few minutes to reduce. Spoon over chicken. Serve immediately with a vegetable garnish and bowls of fruit compote.

TIP

In Holland, a bowl of fruit compote is always on hand to serve with chicken and pork. It is also served with deli cuts. It is well worth trying.

Noisettes de Porc aux Pruneaux

LOIN PORK CHOPS WITH PRUNES AND CREAM SAUCE — FRANCE

INGREDIENTS

12 *Angas Park Pitted Prunes*

¾ cup dry white wine

4 loin pork chops

salt and pepper

½ cup flour

2 tbsp (30g) butter

1 tbsp oil

½ cup chicken stock

½ cup cream

1 tbsp red currant jelly

few drops lemon juice

Place prunes in a bowl and soak in the wine for 4 hours or longer if possible. Place the prunes, with the wine, in a saucepan and simmer gently for 10 minutes or until prunes are tender. Strain the wine from the prunes and set both aside.

Trim chops of fat, season with salt and pepper and dust with flour.

Melt butter with oil in a frying pan. Add chops and brown for 3 minutes each side. Remove from pan.

Drain off almost all the fat from the frying pan, leaving barely enough to cover base of pan. Add wine in which the prunes were cooked and boil briskly, uncovered, until wine has almost evaporated.

Pour in chicken stock, return chops to pan, cover and simmer gently for 30 minutes. Transfer chops to a serving dish and keep warm.

Add cream to frying pan, heat gently, scraping any sediment clinging to sides of pan. Stir in prunes, red currant jelly and lemon juice, heat until jelly has dissolved and prunes are hot.

Correct seasoning and spoon sauce over chops. Serve accompanied with new potatoes and green vegetables.

Serves 4

Jarkoy

BEEF AND FRUIT CASSEROLE — GEORGIA

INGREDIENTS

1kg thick-cut chuck steak*

3 large carrots

3 medium onions, thinly sliced

2 tbsp butter or oil

2 tbsp flour

2 cloves garlic, crushed

1 tsp chopped fresh dill or ½ tsp dried

---

*Chuck steak is ideal for stews and casseroles—it's a sweet-tasting cut which remains juicy. Round or topside steak may be used, but chuck steak gives a better result.

INGREDIENTS CONT.

½ tsp nutmeg, grated or ground

salt and freshly ground black pepper

1½ cups rich beef stock

½ cup *Angas Park Fancy Medium Apricots*

½ cup *Angas Park Peaches*, cut in quarters

½ cup *Angas Park Pitted Prunes*

1 tsp chopped mint

1 tbsp chopped coriander

½ cup walnuts, crushed

¼ cup orange juice

Trim the fat from the chuck steak. Cut into large cubes. Peel and slice the carrots and onions. Heat a large heavy-based saucepan, add butter or oil and a third of the beef cubes. Toss to brown well on all sides over high heat. Remove and brown the remainder in 2 batches. Add the sliced carrot and onions and sauté a little.

Return all meat to saucepan and sprinkle in the flour to cover all the surface. Add the garlic, dill, nutmeg, salt, pepper and beef stock. Bring to the boil over high heat, stirring to lift browned-on juices. Cover, reduce heat to low and simmer slowly for 1½ hours.

After 1½ hours add dried fruits, mint and coriander. Cover and simmer 30 minutes more or until meat is tender. Remove to a heated serving dish. Sprinkle with crushed walnuts and orange juice.

Serves 6

Tomatoes Yemistes

STUFFED TOMATOES — GREECE

INGREDIENTS

12 medium-sized ripe
tomatoes

a little sugar

salt and pepper

½ tsp sugar, extra

½ cup olive oil

1 large onion, finely
chopped

¼ cup pine nuts

1½ cups short grain rice

½ cup *Angas Park
Currants*

1½ cups hot water

2 tbsp chopped
continental parsley

2 tbsp chopped mint

Wash tomatoes. Invert tomatoes to use the top as the base. Tomatoes will sit better in the oven and on the plate. On what is now the "top" of the tomato, make a ¹/₂ cm-thick cut almost to the other side, taking care to leave the "lid" attached.

Flip back the lid and scoop out the pulp with a teaspoon, leaving the walls intact. Sprinkle each cavity with a pinch of sugar, place in a baking dish and set aside.

Place tomato pulp into a saucepan with salt, pepper and ¹/₂ teaspoon sugar, and simmer until pulp is soft. Press through a sieve, rubbing with the back of a wooden spoon. Discard seeds. Set purée aside.

In a saucepan, heat half of the oil (¹/₄ cup) and fry the onion until soft. Add pine nuts and stir 2 minutes. Add rice, stir a little to coat grains with oil, then add currants, hot water, parsley, mint and ¹/₂ cup of the tomato purée. Bring to the boil, turn down heat, cover and simmer gently 10-12 minutes, until all liquid is absorbed.

Spoon rice mixture into tomatoes, allowing a little room for rice to swell. Replace lid. Pour remaining tomato purée over the tomatoes and add about ¹/₂ cup water to the dish.

Spoon remaining oil over the tomatoes and place, uncovered, into a preheated moderate oven for 40 minutes. Check liquid content—if drying out, add a little extra water. However, some tomatoes give out water, which fills the dish. If this is the case, cook for longer to evaporate the water, until tomatoes are surrounded with a thick tomato sauce.

Serve hot or cold. If served cold, allow to cool in the sauce.

TIP

Tomatoes Yemistes taste far better the day after cooking, once the flavours have had time to develop. They may be refrigerated in their baking dish provided it is stainless steel, ovenproof ceramic or glass. Reheat in oven or microwave.

Morg Polou

PERSIAN CHICKEN PILAF — IRAN

INGREDIENTS

1½ cups long grain rice

water for soaking

1 tsp salt

1kg chicken thigh fillets

3 tbsp butter

1 large onion, finely chopped

¼ cup pine nuts

½ tsp chopped fresh thyme

salt and freshly ground black pepper

¼ tsp ground cinnamon

3½ cups hot chicken stock

100g (½ cup) *Angas Park Diced Apricots*

100g (½ cup) *Angas Park Seeded Raisins*

Soak rice in water, with a teaspoon of salt added, for 2 hours. Drain thoroughly. Set aside.

Cut each thigh fillet into 3 or 4 pieces. Heat 2 tablespoons butter in a large, heavy-based saucepan and brown the chicken well on all sides over high heat. Remove to a plate.

Add remaining butter and sauté the onion and pine nuts. Add thyme, salt, pepper and cinnamon. Add the drained rice and stir to coat well with butter. Heat chicken stock to boiling and pour over the rice. Return chicken pieces to saucepan and stir in apricots and raisins. Bring back to the boil for 2 minutes, then lower the heat, cover the saucepan and simmer for 10 minutes.

Place a folded tea towel under the saucepan lid, pressing lid down tightly. Turn down heat to very low and cook for 30-35 minutes undisturbed. Fluff up rice with a fork and serve hot.

Serves 6

TIP

Chicken stock may be made by mixing 3 teaspoons chicken stock powder with 3 cups water.

Spinaci alla Romana

SPINACH WITH RAISINS AND PINE NUTS — SPAIN

INGREDIENTS

3 tbsp *Angas Park Seeded Raisins*

1 bunch English spinach

2 tbsp olive oil

2 tbsp pine nuts

1 medium onion, finely chopped

1 clove garlic, crushed

salt and freshly ground black pepper

Soak raisins in cold water for 15 minutes. Drain well.

Cut off roots from spinach just above the pink tip and wash in 3 changes of water. Shake off excess water and place in a large saucepan. Cover and cook over medium heat until spinach has just wilted. Remove to a colander to cool and drain. Chop spinach roughly.

In a large frying pan, heat 1 tablespoon oil, add pine nuts and cook while stirring until golden. Remove with a slotted spoon. Add remaining tablespoon of oil, onion and garlic, and cook over moderate heat until onion is soft but not coloured.

Add spinach, drained raisins, salt and pepper, and toss gently to heat through. Sprinkle over the pine nuts. Serve hot as a side dish.

Serves 4

Casablanca Chicken

MOROCCO

INGREDIENTS

Chicken

2 tbsp oil

1 tbsp butter

1½ kg chicken pieces

2 large onions, thinly sliced

1 clove garlic, crushed

1 tsp fresh ginger root, chopped

½ tsp turmeric

½ tsp cumin

1 cinnamon stick

½ cup dry white wine

1½ cups apricot nectar (see Tip)

salt and freshly ground black pepper

100g (20) *Angas Park Fancy Medium Prunes*

100g (⅔ cup) *Angas Park Apricots*

1 tbsp honey

¼ cup lemon juice

1 tbsp toasted sesame seeds

Yellow Rice

4 cups chicken stock or water

½ tsp turmeric

1 tsp salt

2 cups long grain rice

Chicken

Heat oil and butter in a large, lidded frying pan, add chicken, a few pieces at a time, and brown well on all sides over high heat. Remove to a plate.

Add onions, reduce heat and fry gently 2 minutes. Add garlic, ginger and spices, and continue to fry for 2 minutes more, stirring to mix ingredients and fry onions evenly.

Return chicken to the pan, stir and turn chicken to coat well with spices.

Add wine and stir to lift pan juices, stir in apricot nectar and season with salt and pepper. Cover and simmer for 30 minutes.

Add prunes, apricots, honey and lemon juice. Cover and simmer 15 minutes more. If liquid content is low, add ¹/₂ cup of apricot nectar or water.

To serve, pile yellow rice on each plate and surround with chicken, fruits and sauce. Sprinkle toasted sesame seeds over chicken. (To toast sesame seeds, place in a heated pan and stir over heat until coloured.)

Yellow Rice

Bring the stock or water to the boil, add turmeric and salt, then slowly add the rice. Stir until it comes back to the boil. Reduce the heat to very low, cover with lid and simmer for 20 minutes, until all liquid is absorbed. Turn off heat and stand, covered, 5 minutes. Fluff up with fork and serve.

TIP

Apricot nectar can be made by boiling ½ cup of dried apricots and 2 cups of water until the apricots are very soft. Purée the apricots and juice together in a blender or pass through a sieve. Add 2 teaspoons of sugar.

Carbonada Griolla

CREOLE-STYLE STEW — ARGENTINA

INGREDIENTS

2 tbsp oil

1 clove garlic, crushed

1 large onion, chopped

1kg boned shoulder of veal, cut into 2cm cubes

1 x 215g can peeled tomatoes

1½ cups beef stock

1 tsp chopped thyme

2 tbsp chopped parsley

INGREDIENTS CONT.

salt and pepper

1 medium potato, cubed

1 sweet potato, cubed

250g pumpkin, cubed

2 fresh corn cobs, cut into thick slices

½ cup short grain rice

4 *Angas Park Peaches*, cut in half

4 *Angas Park Pears*, cut in half

Heat oil in a large saucepan and sauté the garlic and onion. Add veal cubes and quickly stir over high heat to brown lightly.

Add tomatoes, stock, thyme, parsley and season with salt and pepper. Bring to the boil, then turn down heat and simmer for 25 minutes.

Add the cubed vegetables, corn, rice and dried fruits. Cover and simmer for 25 minutes. Stir occasionally during cooking and add extra stock if necessary. Adjust seasoning before serving.

Serves 6

Lamb Korma
LAMB CURRY — INDIA

INGREDIENTS

1½ kg shoulder of lamb

salt and freshly ground black pepper

2 tbsp ghee

1 Spanish onion, finely chopped

1 clove garlic, finely chopped

1 tbsp curry paste

¼ tsp ground ginger

¼ tsp turmeric

⅛ tsp cayenne pepper

INGREDIENTS CONT.

2 tbsp flour

1¼ cups chicken stock

¾ cup (150g) *Angas Park Sultanas*

150ml yoghurt

1 tbsp lemon juice

Cut the lamb from the bone into 4cm cubes. Season with salt and pepper.

Heat ghee in a large, heavy-based saucepan, add ⅓ of the lamb and brown well on all sides. Remove and brown the remainder in 2 batches.

Add the onion and garlic and sauté until transparent. Stir in the curry paste, spices and flour and cook 1 minute. Add the chicken stock, sultanas and lamb. Cover with a lid and simmer gently for 1 hour or until the lamb is very tender. Stir occasionally during cooking.

Stir in the yoghurt and lemon juice. Serve with boiled rice and sambals.

Serves 4-6

Ruaraka

LAMB AND APRICOT STEW — ZANZIBAR

INGREDIENTS

4 ripe tomatoes, blanched and peeled

2 tbsp oil

1 green capsicum, seeded and finely chopped

1 large onion, chopped

2 tbsp fresh mint, chopped

1kg lamb cubes, cut from the leg or shoulder

100g (⅔ cup) *Angas Park Apricots*

salt and freshly ground black pepper

Cut peeled tomatoes in half crosswise (through 'equator'), gently squeeze out seeds and chop the tomato.

Heat half the oil in a heavy-based, lidded frying pan or saucepan, add tomato, capsicum, onion and mint, and sauté 5 minutes. Remove from pan.

Heat remaining oil, add lamb pieces, stir quickly to brown on all sides. Return vegetables to the pan, add the apricots and enough water to almost cover the meat. Bring to the boil, turn down heat and simmer 1 hour.

After the hour season with salt and pepper. Check liquid content and add more if needed. Simmer one hour more, until lamb is very tender. Serve with boiled rice.

Serves 6

Traditional Christmas Pudding with Apricot Rum Butter

ENGLAND

INGREDIENTS

Pudding

250g *Angas Park Currants*

250g *Angas Park Seeded Raisins*

250g *Angas Park Sultanas*

125g *Angas Park Mixed Peel*

50g blanched almonds, chopped

⅓ cup rum

250g treacle

250g butter

1 cup firmly packed brown sugar

4 eggs

2 cups plain flour

1 tsp nutmeg

1 tsp mixed spice

1 tsp cinnamon

1 cup fresh white breadcrumbs

½ tsp bicarbonate of soda dissolved in 1 tbsp warm milk

Apricot Rum Butter

100g (⅔ cup) *Angas Park Apricots*

250g unsalted butter

½ cup icing sugar

2 tbsp ground almonds

1 tbsp rum

½ tsp grated lemon zest

Pudding

Combine dried fruit, almonds and rum in a non-metal container. Cover and leave to stand overnight. Mix treacle into the fruit mixture.

Cream butter and sugar together until light and fluffy. Beat in the eggs, one at a time. Sift the flour and spices together and commence to fold into the butter mixture, alternating with the fruit mixture and breadcrumbs. Lastly, mix in the dissolved bicarbonate of soda.

Pour mixture into a well-greased, 3 litre pudding basin. Cover with a piece of greaseproof paper, greased with butter on both sides, and place the lid on firmly.

Place pudding basin in a boiler with enough boiling water to come half way up the side of the basin. Cover with lid and boil for 5 hours, replenishing water as needed. Keep attending to pudding so as not to boil dry.

When cooked, cool and refrigerate in its basin until needed (up to 4 weeks). To reheat, boil as above for 1 hour. Serve with Apricot Rum Butter.

Apricot Rum Butter

Soak the apricots in water for several hours. Drain and pat dry with kitchen paper. Chop finely.

Beat butter until white and fluffy with an electric mixer. Beat in icing sugar, almonds, rum and lemon zest. Add chopped apricots and beat to mix well.

Pile into pots and refrigerate until required. Alternatively, place teaspoonful-sized mounds onto an oven tray and refrigerate until set. When set, remove from to a covered container and store in refrigerator until required. Serve with hot Christmas pudding.

Something Vegetarian

Angas Park dried fruits are a valuable ingredient in the vegetarian diet. As well as increasing the protein content of a meal, they add texture and flavour. In this chapter, new ideas for vegetarian meals will also excite non-vegetarians.

Photographed from left: Brandied Raisins and Broccoli Salad, recipe page 70; Burghul Pilaf, recipe page 70.

69

Brandied Raisins and Broccoli Salad

INGREDIENTS

Salad

100g (¾ cup) *Angas Park Seeded Raisins*

3 tbsp brandy

pinch of salt

500g broccoli, cut into florets

1 mignonette lettuce, washed and crisped

2 large carrots, sliced into ribbons with potato peeler

2 tbsp flaked almonds, toasted

Place the raisins and brandy in a screw-top jar. Shake well and leave to marinate several hours or overnight. Shake the jar occasionally.

Bring a large saucepan of water to the boil, add a good pinch of salt. Add broccoli and boil rapidly until broccoli turns a bright green colour and softens a little (about 2 minutes). Drain immediately and plunge into iced water for a few minutes. Drain broccoli well, pat dry with kitchen paper.

To crisp the lettuce leaves, rinse in a colander under running water, drain well, shake dry in a clean tea towel and place in the refrigerator wrapped in the damp towel.

Drain the raisins, reserve brandy for other uses. Toss broccoli, carrot ribbons and raisins together and place in a shallow salad bowl or platter lined with lettuce leaves.

Mix all dressing ingredients together and pour over salad. Sprinkle with toasted, flaked almonds.

INGREDIENTS CONT.

Dressing

3 tbsp mayonnaise

2 tbsp plain yoghurt

1 tbsp cider vinegar

1 tsp honey

¼ tsp salt

freshly ground black pepper

Burghul Pilaf

INGREDIENTS

2 tbsp butter

1 stalk celery, finely chopped

1 small onion, finely chopped

1 cup burghul

2 cups vegetable stock or water

Melt butter in a saucepan and sauté the celery and onion until softened. Stir in the burghul and coat with the melted butter. Add the stock or water, salt and pepper to taste. Bring to the boil, cover and simmer 10 minutes.

Add apricots, raisins and pine nuts, cover and continue cooking 10-15 minutes, or until burghul is soft and fluffy and water has absorbed. Turn off heat and stand, covered, for 5 minutes. Pile into a serving dish, fluff up with a fork.

INGREDIENTS CONT.

salt and freshly ground black pepper

10 *Angas Park Apricots*

1 tbsp *Angas Park Seeded Raisins*

2 tbsp pine nuts, toasted

Spinach Risotto with Raisins and Almonds

INGREDIENTS

1 bunch English spinach

2 tbsp oil

½ bunch shallots, chopped

⅔ cup rice

1¾ cups hot water

salt and freshly ground black pepper

3 tbsp lemon juice

100g (¾ cup) *Angas Park Seeded Raisins*

50g almonds, blanched and toasted

Trim roots from the spinach just above the pink tip. Wash in 3-4 changes of cold water. Drain well and chop roughly.

Heat oil in a saucepan, add shallots and sauté a little. Add rice and stir until coated with oil and rice has coloured slightly, about 30 seconds.

Add spinach, hot water, salt, pepper and lemon juice. Cover and cook on medium heat 10 minutes. Remove lid, stir to combine, add raisins, re-cover and cook 5 minutes more. Turn off heat and stand, covered, 5 minutes before serving to plump the rice. Sprinkle with almonds. Serve with crusty bread.

Serves 3

Peach and Asparagus Salad

INGREDIENTS

Salad

1 x 200g packet *Angas Park Peaches*

¼ cup lemon juice

2 tbsp olive oil

1 clove garlic, crushed

1 long, thin French bread stick

2 bunches (500g) fresh asparagus

1 cos lettuce

1 mignonette lettuce

2 avocados, cut into large dice

1 tbsp toasted sesame seeds (see Tip)

Citrus Dressing

1 tsp grated orange zest

⅓ cup orange juice

1 tsp grated lemon zest

1 tbsp lemon juice

2 tbsp mayonnaise

2 tbsp olive oil

1 tbsp balsamic vinegar

2 tsp sugar

Salad

Place peaches in a shallow plate and drizzle with ¼ cup of lemon juice. Cover and stand until ready to use.

Tear the larger leaves of the cos lettuce into smaller pieces and separate the inner, tender leaves. Combine with the mignonette lettuce leaves. Rinse in a colander under running water, drain well, shake dry in a clean tea towel and place in the refrigerator wrapped in the damp towel to crisp.

Mix olive oil and garlic together. Cut bread stick into ½ cm diagonal slices. Brush both sides with the garlic oil, place on a flat baking tray and bake in a moderate oven 170°C for 15 minutes, until golden and crisp. Turn over half way through baking. Remove and set aside.

Trim coarse fibre from ends of asparagus with a potato peeler and cut each in 3 pieces. Boil in a saucepan of boiling water for 1 minute, refresh in cold water and drain well.

Place lettuce leaves in a large salad bowl or platter. Toss in the asparagus, avocado, peaches and bread slices. Pour over the dressing (see below), toss gently. Sprinkle with toasted sesame seeds.

Citrus Dressing

Whisk all ingredients together in a bowl or process in a food processor or blender.

Serves 6

TIP

To toast sesame seeds, heat a small pan, add sesame seeds and stir over heat until golden. Remove immediately from pan and cool.

Curried Vegetables

INGREDIENTS

500g small chat potatoes, cut in half

4 tbsp oil

400g onions, peeled and thinly sliced

250g green zucchini, cut in 2cm-thick rounds

250g yellow squash, cut in half

250g stringless beans, topped, tailed and cut in half

3 tbsp butter or ghee

2 tbsp curry paste

INGREDIENTS CONT.

¾ cup *Angas Park Seeded Raisins*, soaked for 10 minutes

1 red capsicum, cut in 2cm squares

50g pistachio nuts, chopped

1 tbsp sunflower seeds (optional)

Boil the potatoes in boiling, salted water until just tender. Drain and set aside. Heat oil in a frying pan, add the onions and toss to coat with oil. Reduce heat, cover and allow to cook on low heat until onions become soft. Remove lid, increase heat and fry, stirring frequently until the onions are well browned. Drain on kitchen paper.

Par boil the zucchini, squash and beans in boiling, salted water for 2 minutes. Drain and immediately cover with cold water. Leave 30 seconds, then drain well.

Heat butter or ghee in a large frying pan, add curry paste and cook, stirring, until fragrant. Add potatoes, cook, tossing around the pan until brown and crisp. Add par-boiled vegetables, raisins and capsicum. Stir fry to heat through and coat with curry paste. Toss through the pistachio nuts and sunflower seeds. Remove to a serving platter and top with the fried onions. Serve hot.

Serves 4-5

Indian Rice

INGREDIENTS

1½ cups basmati rice

4 cups water

½ tsp salt

2 tbsp lemon juice

2 tbsp ghee

1 medium Spanish onion, chopped

3 tbsp cashew nuts

3 tbsp *Angas Park Sultanas*

¼ tsp fennel seeds

¼ tsp cumin seeds

INGREDIENTS CONT.

¼ tsp white mustard seeds

¼ tsp ground turmeric

1 tsp ghee, extra

Rinse rice well in a sieve under running water. Bring 4 cups of water to boil, add salt and lemon juice. Stir in the rice and, when water returns to the boil, turn down the heat and simmer 18 minutes, until rice is just tender. Drain in colander and rinse with hot water. Set aside.

Heat ghee in a large frying pan. Add onion and cook until transparent. Add cashews and sultanas and sauté a little. Add spices and extra teaspoon of ghee and cook, stirring constantly, for 2 minutes.

Add drained rice, gently toss to combine ingredients and reheat the rice. Serve hot with curries or serve as a side dish with grilled meats and chicken.

Serves 4

Rice and Apricot Pilaf

INGREDIENTS

3 tbsp oil or butter

1 large onion, finely chopped

1½ cups rice

3½ cups hot water

salt and freshly ground pepper

2 tbsp parsley, finely chopped

2 tbsp lemon juice

1 x 200g packet *Angas Park Apricots*

2 tbsp *Angas Park Seeded Raisins*

50g almonds, blanched and toasted (see Tip)

In a large saucepan heat oil or butter and fry the onion until pale golden in colour. Add the rice and stir 30 seconds to coat with oil.

Add the hot water, salt, pepper, lemon juice and parsley. Cover and simmer for 10 minutes.

Stir in the apricots (whole), raisins and almonds and simmer for 5 minutes more. Remove from heat and allow to stand, covered, for 5 minutes before serving to plump the rice.

Serve hot with a side salad.

Serves 4

TIP

Quick toasted almonds: melt 2 teaspoons of butter on a plate in the microwave for 10 seconds, add almonds and stir to coat with butter. Microwave on high for 2-3 minutes, stirring each minute, until pale golden. Cool.

Tofu with Peaches and Snow Peas

INGREDIENTS

375g tub of tofu

½ cup flour, seasoned with salt and pepper

3 tbsp oil

1 large onion, cut into thin rings

1cm piece fresh ginger root, peeled

1 clove garlic

300g snow peas, topped and tailed

⅓ cup dry white wine (if not available, use white vinegar)

1 x 200g packet *Angas Park Peaches*

3 tsp soy sauce

2 tsp sugar

2 tsp fresh ginger juice (see Tip on page 19)

Cut tofu into 6 cubes. Pat dry with kitchen paper. Coat with seasoned flour, shake off excess.

Heat oil in a large frying pan and fry onion rings until golden. Remove with slotted spoon or tongs and drain on kitchen paper.

To the oil in the pan add the ginger and garlic, fry for 30 seconds to flavour the oil, remove. Add tofu cubes and fry until golden on all sides, turning with tongs. Adjust heat as needed. Remove and drain on kitchen paper, keep hot.

Pour the oil from the pan, taking care not to include the flour sediment. Wipe pan clean with kitchen paper. Return about 1 tablespoon of oil to the pan, add snow peas and stir fry 1 minute or to desired crispness. Remove to a plate.

Pour wine into pan and place in the peaches, in a single layer. Simmer 1 minute, turn peaches. Add soy sauce, sugar and ginger juice. Swirl pan to mix. Heat through.

Pile snow peas on serving plates. Arrange tofu cubes and peaches on and around snow peas, pour over the sauce and top with onion rings.

Serves 2-3

TIP

English spinach or baby bok choy can be used in place of snow peas.

Something Sweet

The use of dried fruits in puddings, desserts, cakes, biscuits and pies is well known. The softer texture and richer flavour of Angas Park dried fruits contribute to their success.

Photographed from bottom left, clockwise: Fruit and Nut Chocolate Clusters, page 80; Peach Cobbler, recipe page 81; Dried Fruit Salad, recipe page 80; Rich Bread Pudding with Sultanas, recipe page 81.

Fruit and Nut Chocolate Clusters

INGREDIENTS

200g dark compound chocolate, melted

150g *Angas Park Seeded Raisins*

150g *Angas Park Sultanas*

100g mixed, chopped nuts

Place 2 sheets of baking paper or foil on 2 flat trays.

Break chocolate into squares and place in a heatproof bowl. Set the bowl over a saucepan of simmering water. Do not allow the bottom of the bowl to touch the water, and do not allow steam or moisture to contact the chocolate. When chocolate begins to melt, turn off heat. Stir chocolate until it melts to pouring consistency.

Remove bowl from saucepan and set in dish of warm water. Stir in raisins, sultanas and nuts. Mix well, then drop teaspoonfuls onto the prepared tray.

Allow to set at room temperature to retain the chocolate's shine.

TIP

Many combinations of *Angas Park* fruits may be used to make clusters.

Dried Fruit Salad

INGREDIENTS

250g *Angas Park Fancy Medium Apricots*

150g *Angas Park Pitted Prunes*

100g *Angas Park Seeded Raisins*

100g *Angas Park Peaches*, cut in half

1 tbsp lemon juice

½ cup slivered almonds

strip of lemon zest

Place all ingredients, except the zest, in a large glass or china bowl. Add enough water to cover (about 2-3 cups), cover with plastic wrap and stand several hours or overnight. The fruit will plump and soften, and the flavours will blend.

Strain soaking liquid into a saucepan, return fruit to the bowl. Add a strip of lemon zest. Bring liquid to the boil and continue to boil until reduced by half and has formed a syrup. Cool and pour back over fruit. Chill well before serving.

Serve chilled with yoghurt or cream.

TIP

This dish is sweetened by natural fruit juices reduced to a syrup. If extra sweetness is desired, add 1 tablespoon of sugar to the fruit.

Rich Bread Pudding with Sultanas

INGREDIENTS

2 eggs, separated

2 tbsp soft butter

⅔ cup sugar

1 cup fresh white
breadcrumbs

pinch of salt

300ml cream

½ cup milk

1 tsp vanilla essence

grated zest and juice of
1 lemon

50g (2 tbsp) *Angas Park
Sultanas*

lightly whipped cream,
for serving

Lightly grease a 2 litre soufflé dish or other heatproof, deep dish. Beat together the egg yolks, soft butter and sugar until smooth and creamy. Stir in the breadcrumbs, salt, cream and milk.

Pour mixture into a saucepan and heat gently, while stirring, until the mixture begins to thicken. Remove from the heat and add the vanilla, lemon zest and juice. Stir in the sultanas and mix well.

Stiffly beat the egg whites and gently fold into the mixture. Pour into the prepared dish. Stand in a baking pan containing hot water, 3cm deep.

Place in a preheated oven 170°C and bake for 35-40 minutes, until well risen, firm to touch and golden. Serve warm with lightly whipped cream, if desired.

Peach Cobbler

INGREDIENTS

1 x 200g packet *Angas
Park Peaches*

¾ cup water

2 tbsp sugar

90g butter

½ cup sugar, extra

½ tsp vanilla essence

2 eggs, beaten

1¼ cups self raising flour

¼ cup milk

Place peaches in a small saucepan, add water and stand to soak 10 minutes. Bring to the boil, stir in sugar and cook gently until soft, about 10 minutes. Place peaches and syrup into a greased ovenproof dish.

Cream together the butter and extra sugar until fluffy. Add vanilla and beat in the eggs, a little at a time. Fold in the sifted flour and milk, stir lightly until all is incorporated. Pour over the peaches.

Bake in a moderate oven at 180°C for 30-35 minutes, until cake topping is cooked.

Serve warm with cream or custard.

TIP

Apricots or a mixture of dried fruits may be used in place of peaches.

Sultana and Orange Cake

INGREDIENTS

250g unsalted butter

¾ cup caster sugar

3 eggs, lightly beaten

100g (¾ cup) *Angas Park Sultanas*

1¼ cups self raising flour

⅔ cup rice flour

1 tbsp grated orange zest

⅓ cup orange juice

Grease a 23 x 13 x 7cm loaf tin with butter and line with greased paper cut to fit. Beat butter and sugar together until light and fluffy. Gradually beat in the eggs and add the sultanas.

Sift the 2 flours together. Fold into the mixture with a large metal spoon, adding the zest and orange juice as you fold.

Spoon mixture into prepared tin and bake in a preheated moderate oven 180°C for 45-50 minutes or until a skewer inserted into the centre of the cake comes out clean. Allow cake to cool for 10 minutes before turning out onto cake cooler. Dust with icing sugar and serve.

Sticky Peach Pudding with Caramel Balsamic Sauce

INGREDIENTS

Pudding

1 x 200g packet *Angas Park Peaches*

¾ cup water

60g butter

¾ cup sugar

1 tsp vanilla essence

2 eggs

1½ cups self raising flour, sifted

INGREDIENTS CONT.

Sauce

90g butter

¾ cup brown sugar

¾ cup cream

1 tbsp balsamic vinegar

Pudding

Grease a 20cm square cake tin and line base with greaseproof paper. Grease the paper. Chop the peaches, place in a saucepan with the water and bring to the boil. Boil 1 minute. Remove from heat and set aside to cool.

Cream butter and sugar together until light and fluffy, add vanilla. Beat in eggs, a little at a time, and stir in the peaches plus juice. Fold in the flour. Pour into the prepared tin. Bake in a moderate oven 180°C for 35-40 minutes. Turn out, cool slightly. Cut into squares. Serve warm with Caramel Balsamic Sauce. (The peach pudding can be made in advance. Reheat to warm in a slow oven for 10 minutes before cutting.)

Caramel Balsamic Sauce

Melt butter in a saucepan over low heat. Stir in the brown sugar and cook until bubbly. Add the cream and stir until smooth. Stir in the vinegar.

Serve warm.

Frozen Christmas Pudding

INGREDIENTS

75g (½ cup) *Angas Park Pitted Prunes*, chopped

1 x 200g packet *Angas Park Fruit Medley*

100g (⅔ cup) *Angas Park Currants*

150g (1 cup) *Angas Park Seeded Raisins*, chopped

¼ cup *Angas Park Mixed Peel*

½ -¾ cup rum

⅓ cup almonds, blanched, toasted and chopped

125g dark chocolate, grated coarsely

Soak the dried fruits overnight in the rum, in a glass bowl covered with plastic wrap. Fold almonds and chocolate through fruit. Soften the ice cream by standing at room temperature for ¹/₂ hour. (or place in microwave for 20-30 seconds, stand 2 minutes.) Mix into the fruit and rum mixture. Fold in whipped cream.

Line a pudding basin or large mixing bowl, preferably metal or enamel, with plastic wrap, leaving an overhang (use 2 pieces of plastic, one placed north/south, the other east/west). Place ice cream mixture into the bowl. Cover with plastic wrap and freeze for 36 hours or more.

Loosen the pudding by pulling on the plastic wrap overhang, fold back the wrap and invert onto serving platter. Peel off the wrap. Decorate with extra whipped cream. Return to freezer until serving time.

Serves 12

INGREDIENTS CONT.

2 litres vanilla ice cream

300ml thickened cream, whipped

extra cream, whipped, for decoration

Peach Blossom Cake

INGREDIENTS

Peach Filling

1 x 200g packet *Angas Park Peaches*

1½ cups boiling water

½ cup sugar

2 tbsp lemon juice

Cake

1½ cups self raising flour

½ cup caster sugar

60g butter, cut in pieces

1 egg

1 tsp vanilla essence

Peach Filling

Place peaches in a saucepan and add the boiling water. Stand to soak 10 minutes. Place on heat and simmer, covered, for 10 minutes, or until soft. Cool slightly and purée in a blender or food processor. Return purée to saucepan, add sugar and lemon juice. Stir over heat for 3-5 minutes. Add a little extra water if necessary. Allow the mixture to bubble a little. Cool well.

Cake

Sift flour into a bowl, add sugar and mix. Add butter and rub into the flour with fingertips until it is crumbly. Add the egg and vanilla, and mix to a stiff dough.

Grease a 20cm springform tin or deep cake tin with butter. Line base with greased greaseproof paper cut to size. With floured hand, press about ²/₃ of the dough into the prepared tin. Keep dipping fingers in flour when they stick.

Spread peach filling over the dough. Drop small pieces of dough over the peach filling, using 2 teaspoons.

Bake in a preheated oven 180°C for 30-35 minutes or until golden brown.

Allow to cool a little. Run a round-bladed knife around edge to loosen. Release spring ring and slide off base onto a cake cooler. Remove paper. If using a plain cake tin, invert onto a plate. Remove paper and invert onto a cake cooler.

TIP

The cake mixture may be made in a food processor: place flour and sugar in processor bowl and, with motor running, drop in butter pieces. Then add the egg and process until crumbly. Transfer to a bowl and use your hands to press into a dough ball.

Rum and Raisin Pie

INGREDIENTS

Crumb Crust

125g plain sweet biscuits, crushed

1 tsp ground cinnamon

60g butter, melted

Filling

1 cup hot water

100g (¾ cup) *Angas Park Seeded Raisins*

1 tbsp rum

250g cream cheese

1 cup caster sugar

3 eggs

Crumb Crust

Combine crushed biscuits, cinnamon and melted butter together. Press into the sides and base of a 20cm springform tin or 23cm flan tin with a removable base. Chill in the refrigerator.

Filling

Mix hot water and raisins together, allow to soak for ½-1 hour. Drain well and add rum. Stand for at least 20 minutes. Beat the cream cheese and sugar together until fluffy. Beat in eggs, one at a time. Stir in the rum and raisins.

Pour into the crumb-lined tin. Bake in moderate oven 180°C for 20-25 minutes. Allow to cool, refrigerate for several hours. Remove from springform tin. Trim edges of crumb crust and dust with a layer of icing sugar.

TIP

To decorate, heat metal skewers over a gas flame or in the oven and press in a criss-cross pattern onto the icing sugar.

Alternatively, heat a wire cake cooler and press onto the surface. This will scorch the icing sugar, creating a decorative pattern.

Something Saucy

Flavour, consistency and variety are the qualities dried fruits offer to sauce-making. With the addition of dried fruit-based sauces, a simple grill, barbecue or cold meat platter will be more exciting, and ice cream becomes an exotic dessert.

Chilli and Sultana Sauce

INGREDIENTS

2 tbsp chilli powder

200ml white vinegar

2 cloves garlic, crushed

Place all ingredients in a saucepan and bring to the boil. Reduce heat and simmer gently until sultanas are very soft, about 10 minutes.

Cool, then place in a food processor or blender and process until smooth. For a smoother sauce, rub through a fine sieve. Pour into sterilised bottles (see Tip on page 89) and seal. Serve with barbecued and grilled meats.

INGREDIENTS CONT.

1 tsp freshly grated ginger

1½ cups sugar

200g *Angas Park Sultanas*

1½ tsp salt

Raisin Sauce

INGREDIENTS

¾ cup sugar

¾ cup water

150g (1 cup) *Angas Park Seeded Raisins*, cut in halves

1 tbsp Worcestershire sauce

½ tsp Tabasco sauce

Place sugar and water in a saucepan. Heat to boiling, stirring to dissolve all sugar. Add all remaining ingredients except the arrowroot. Simmer for 10 minutes.

Add the blended arrowroot and stir until sauce boils and thickens. Serve hot with roast turkey, hot, thick-sliced ham or ham steaks, pork chops or any grilled meats or chicken.

INGREDIENTS CONT.

⅛ tsp nutmeg

2 tsp butter

2 tbsp wine vinegar

salt and freshly ground black pepper

½ cup red currant jelly

1 tbsp arrowroot, blended with 1 tbsp water

Jamaican Fruit Sauce

INGREDIENTS

1 x 200g *Angas Park Fruit Salad*

½ cup hot water

2 tbsp butter

½ cup brown sugar

Cut larger fruits into 2 or 3 pieces. Place in a bowl and add the hot water, allow to soak 20 minutes. Melt butter in a saucepan over moderate heat. Add brown sugar and stir until butter and sugar are well combined and bubbly. Stir in the fruits and soaking liquid. Simmer for 3-5 minutes.

Stir in the rum and nuts, and continue to simmer until the liquid becomes a syrupy consistency. Remove to a serving bowl. Serve warm over ice cream, steamed pudding, baked custards or other deserts.

INGREDIENTS CONT.

4 tbsp rum

50g Brazil nuts

25g blanched almonds or cashew nuts

Prune and Raisin Sauce

INGREDIENTS

100g (15) *Angas Park Pitted Prunes*

50g (2 tbsp) *Angas Park Seeded Raisins*

1 tbsp finely chopped onion

²⁄₃ cup water

50ml (2½ tbsp) malt vinegar

Place prunes, raisins, onion and water in a saucepan. Bring to the boil, then simmer for 5 minutes. Add remaining ingredients, except cream, and simmer 5 minutes more. Cool a little.

Pour mixture into a blender or food processor and process until a smooth purée. Return purée to saucepan, stir in the cream and reheat over low heat, stirring occasionally. Serve hot with pork, veal or lamb either grilled, pan-fried or roasted.

Makes approx. 1½ cups

INGREDIENTS CONT.

2 tsp sugar

¼ tsp nutmeg

1 tsp mustard powder *or* 1½ tsp prepared mustard

2 tsp Worcestershire sauce

½ cup cream

Quick Citrus Marmalade

INGREDIENTS

1 x 200g packet *Angas Park Mixed Peel*

2½ cups water

3 cups sugar

¼ cup lemon juice

Place mixed peel and water into a saucepan and boil, covered, until peel is soft, about 20-25 minutes.

Add sugar and lemon juice, stir to dissolve sugar. Boil, uncovered, at a moderate pace, about 30 minutes, until the setting point is reached (see below). Allow to cool slightly and pour into a warm, sterilised jar (see Tip). Seal with lid when completely cold.

To test for setting point, drop a teaspoon of marmalade onto a chilled plate and allow to cool (can be put into refrigerator to speed up cooling). If, once cooled, the skin that forms on the top wrinkles when touched, setting point has been reached. Remember to remove saucepan from heat while conducting this test.

Makes 2½ cups

TIP

To sterilise jars: wash and rinse jars and place in a boiler of cold water to cover. Bring to the boil and boil for 5 minutes. Remove and overturn to drain and air dry. Place in a low oven to dry completely and keep warm prior to bottling.

Microwave method: fill washed jars with water and bring to the boil in the microwave on high power. Drain well.

Rich Apricot Sauce

INGREDIENTS

1 x 200g packet *Angas Park Fancy Large Apricots*

2 cups water

2 tbsp butter

4 tbsp brown sugar

2-3 tbsp brandy or whisky

Place apricots and water in a saucepan, stand to soak 10 minutes. Place over heat and cook until apricots are very soft. Cool a little and purée, with its liquid, in a blender or food processor.

Melt butter in a clean saucepan, add brown sugar and cook while stirring until well combined and bubbling. Do not allow butter to separate from mixture with overcooking. Add apricot purée and stir to combine and heat through. Stir in brandy or whisky.

Place in a bowl. Allow to come to a warm temperature before serving. Serve warm over ice cream or other desserts.

Makes 3 cups

TIP

This sauce is designed to be served warm. However, it may be stored in the refrigerator or freezer and warmed in a microwave for 40 seconds before serving.

Barbecue Sauce with Apricot

INGREDIENTS

120g (¾ cup) *Angas Park Diced Apricots*

1½ cups hot water

1 tbsp oil

1 large onion, finely chopped

2 cloves garlic, crushed

3 tbsp wine vinegar

2 tbsp brown sugar

Soak apricots in the hot water for 1 hour.

Heat oil in a saucepan and gently fry the onion and garlic until soft, but not coloured. Add soaked apricots and their juice, and bring to the boil.

When boiling, turn down heat and add all remaining ingredients. Simmer for 10 minutes, until apricots are soft.

Cool a little, then purée in a food processor or blender. Serve hot or cold with your favourite barbecue foods or grills.

INGREDIENTS CONT.

1 tsp Mexican-style chilli powder

½ tsp Tabasco sauce

½ tsp salt

½ tsp pepper

1 tbsp Worcestershire sauce

¼ cup lemon juice

Dried Apricot Jam

INGREDIENTS

1 x 200g packet *Angas Park Diced Apricots*

3 cups water

2 tbsp lemon juice

2½ cups sugar

Place apricots in a strainer and rinse under running water. Place in a bowl, add water and allow to soak for many hours or overnight.

Place apricots and soaking water in a saucepan. Bring to the boil, turn down heat to moderate, cover and cook 20 minutes, until apricots are very soft. Add lemon juice and sugar, stir until all sugar is dissolved. Reduce heat and simmer, uncovered, until setting point is reached, about 30 minutes. Stir occasionally to make sure it is not catching on the bottom (jam may be cooked more rapidly, but it is more likely to catch on the bottom).

As soon as setting point is reached (see Tip), remove from the heat. Allow to cool enough to place in warm, sterilised jars (see Tip on page 89 for sterilisation method).

Makes 3 cups

TIP

To test for setting point: drop a teaspoon of jam or marmalade onto a chilled plate and allow to cool (can be put in refrigerator). If the skin which forms on the top wrinkles when touched, the setting point has been reached. Remember to remove saucepan from heat while conducting this test.

Weights and Measures

English and American Measures

English

All measurements are similar to Australian with two exceptions: **(i)** the English cup measures 10 fluid ounces (300ml), whereas the Australian cup measures 8 fluid ounces (250ml); and **(ii)** the English tablespoon (the Australian dessertspoon) measures 14.8ml against the Australian tablespoon of 20ml.

American

The American reputed pint is 16 fluid ounces, a quart is equal to 32 fluid ounces, and the American gallon is 128 fluid ounces. The Imperial measurement is 20 fluid ounces to the pint, 40 fluid ounces to the quart, and 160 fluid ounces to one gallon. The American tablespoon is equal to 14.8ml, and the teaspoon is 5ml. The cup measure is 8 fluid ounces (250ml), the same as in Australia.

Dry Measures

All the measures are level, so when you have filled a cup or spoon, level it off with the edge of a knife. *The scale below is the "cook's equivalent", and is not an exact conversion of metric to imperial measurement.* The exact metric equivalent is 2.2046 lb = 1kg, or 1 lb = 0.45359kg

METRIC		IMPERIAL	
g = grams		oz = ounces	
kg = kilograms		lb = pound	
15g		$^1/_2$ oz	
20g		$^2/_3$ oz	
30g		1 oz	
60g		2 oz	
90g		3 oz	
125g		4 oz	$^1/_4$ lb
155g		5 oz	
185g		6 oz	
220g		7 oz	
250g		8 oz	$^1/_2$ lb
280g		9 oz	
315g		10 oz	
345g		11 oz	
375g		12 oz	$^3/_4$ lb
410g		13 oz	
440g		14 oz	
470g		15 oz	
1000g	1kg	35.2 oz	2.2 lb
	1.5kg		3.3 lb

Cup Meaures

One cup is equal to the following weights.

	METRIC	IMPERIAL
Almonds, flaked	90g	3 oz
Almonds, slivered, ground	125g	4 oz
Almonds, kernels	155g	5 oz
Apples, dried, chopped	125g	4 oz
Apricots, dried, chopped	190g	6 oz
Breadcrumbs, packet	125g	4 oz
Breadcumbs, soft	60g	2 oz
Cheese, grated	125g	4 oz
Choc Bits	155g	5 oz
Coconut, desiccated	90g	3 oz
Cornflakes	30g	1 oz
Currants	155g	5 oz
Flour	125g	4 oz
Fruit, dried (mixed, sultanas etc.)	185g	6 oz
Ginger, crystallised, glacé	250g	8 oz
Honey, treacle, golden syrup	315g	10 oz
Mixed Peel	220g	7 oz
Nuts, chopped	125g	4 oz
Prunes, chopped	220g	7 oz
Rice, cooked	155g	5 oz
Rice, uncooked	185g	6 oz
Rolled Oats	90g	3 oz
Sesame Seeds	125g	4 oz
Shortening (butter, margarine)	250g	8 oz
Sugar, brown	155g	5 oz
Sugar, granulated or caster	250g	8 oz
Sugar, sifted icing	155g	5 oz
Wheat germ	60g	2 oz

Liquid Measures

METRIC ml (millilitres)	IMPERIAL fl oz (fluid ounces)	CUP & SPOON
5ml	$^1/_6$ fl oz	1 teaspoon
20ml	$^2/_3$ fl oz	1 tablespoon
30ml	1 fl oz	1 tablespoon plus 2 teaspoons
60ml	2 fl oz	$^1/_4$ cup
85ml	$2^1/_2$ fl oz	$^1/_3$ cup
100ml	3 fl oz	$^3/_8$ cup
125ml	4 fl oz	$^1/_2$ cup
150ml	5 fl oz	$^1/_4$ pint, 1 gill
250ml	8 fl oz	1 cup
300ml	10 fl oz	$^1/_2$ pint
360ml	12 fl oz	$1^1/_2$ cups
420ml	14 fl oz	$1^3/_4$ cups
500ml	16 fl oz	2 cups
600ml	20 fl oz	1 pint, $2^1/_2$ cups
1 litre	35 fl oz	$1^3/_4$ pints, 4 cups

Length

Some of us are still having trouble converting imperial to metric. In this scale, measures have been rounded off to the easiest-to-use and most acceptable figures.

To obtain the exact metric equivalent when converting inches to centimetres, multiply inches by 2.54. Therefore, 1 inch equals 25.4 millimetres and 1 millimetre equals 0.03937 inches.

METRIC mm = millimetres cm = centimetres	IMPERIAL in = inches ft = feet
5mm (0.5cm)	$^1/_4$ in
10mm (1.0cm)	$^1/_2$ in
20mm (2.0cm)	$^3/_4$ in
25mm (2.5cm)	1 in
50mm (5cm)	2 in
80mm (8cm)	3 in
100mm (10cm)	4 in
120mm (12cm)	5 in
150mm (15cm)	6 in
180mm (18cm)	7 in
200mm (20cm)	8 in
230mm (23cm)	9 in
250mm (25cm)	10 in
280mm (28cm)	11 in
300mm (30cm)	1 ft (12 in)

Oven Temperatures

The Celsius temperatures given here are not exact; they have been rounded off and are given as a guide only. Follow the manufacturer's temperature guide, relating it to oven description given in the recipe.

Remember gas ovens are hottest at the top, electric ovens at the bottom and convection fan-forced ovens are usually even throughout. We include Regulo numbers for gas cookers which may assist. To convert °C to °F, multiply °C by 9 and divide by 5, then add 32.

	°C	°F	REGULO
Very slow	120	250	1
Slow	150	300	2
Moderately slow	150	325	3
Moderate	180	350	4
Moderately hot	190–200	370–400	5–6
Hot	210–220	410–440	6–7
Very hot	230	450	8
Super hot	250–290	475–500	9–10

Cake Dish Sizes

METRIC	IMPERIAL
15cm	6"
18cm	7"
20cm	8"
23cm	9"

Loaf Dish Sizes

METRIC	IMPERIAL
23cm x 12cm	9" x 5"
25cm x 8cm	10" x 3"
28cm x 18cm	11" x 7"

Index

Notes